HISTORY

A

KI

CHIL

Other titles in the **Key Strategies** series:

PLANNING PRIMARY
HISTORY

FOR THE REVISED NATIONAL CURRICULUM

KS KEY STRATEGIES

**Key Stages
1 & 2**

**Tim Lomas, Christine Burke
Dave Cordingley, Karen McKenzie
Lesley Tyreman**

JOHN MURRAY

Cover Photograph: By courtesy of Peter Newark's Pictures

Acknowledgements:
Page 37: Baby's Birthday, 1867 by Frederick Daniel Hardy
Wolverhampton Art Gallery/ Bridgeman Art Library, London

First published in 1996
by John Murray (Publishers) Ltd
50 Albemarle Street, London W1X 4BD

Reprinted 1997

Layout by Christine Archer
Typeset in 10 ½/12pt Rockwell by Wearset, Boldon, Tyne and Wear
Printed and bound in Great Britain by St Edmundsbury Press, Bury St Edmunds

A catalogue entry for this title can be obtained from the British Library

ISBN 0 7195 7054 9

Contents

The revised National Curriculum for History

1.1 Good practice

What do we mean by good practice in primary history? Ask any group of teachers to define it and the range of responses will be very varied. It will be more varied still if parents, the government, advisers or OFSTED inspectors are asked.

However, in this book we argue strongly that the following should be in any list of characteristics of good practice:

1 **A variety of teaching and learning approaches,** including whole class work, group and individual tasks, and using different media: writing, reading, speaking, listening, watching, information technology, fieldwork and the use of a wide range of sources.

2 **Work which interests pupils:** familiar and personal history such as local and family history; linking past times to familiar and personal issues; practical work such as fieldwork using artefacts; drama and films; investigations; detective work; decision-making activities; opportunities for pupils to be adventurous; creative and imaginative work; depth work; stories involving human beings. Pupils will not be stimulated if there is too great a use of assessment activity.

3 **A clear framework providing some coherence** to the history experience. This framework should ensure coverage of the full range of historical content, skills and concepts; it should foster links between study units; it should include regular exposure to historical learning; it should ensure that history lessons have a logical structure.

4 **A clear progression** in historical competence. Teachers should be aware of the characteristics of progression in history and ways in which pupils' competence can be developed. There should not be slavish adherence to statements of attainment or banding definitions.

5 **Balance.** This is partly determined by the requirements of the National Curriculum, especially in Key Stage 2, but teachers should ensure that there is a reasonable balance of time periods, geographical areas (local, national and global) and perspectives (political, social, etc.).

6 **Appropriate work for all pupils.** Most primary classes have a wide range of ability (and sometimes age). Pupils are capable of high levels of historical understanding even at a young age, and it is important to challenge pupils at their own level of understanding and to keep expectations of all pupils high.

7 **Good teacher expertise.** Ideally teachers should have a good background knowledge of the topics being covered and access to

interesting stories and anecdotes to enhance history teaching, and should be confident in the use of a range of learning methods.

8 **Good classroom management strategies.** These should include a good range of pupil experiences, clear instructions and explanations, good monitoring of progress and a positive and pleasant atmosphere.

9 **A well-organised curriculum area**, well coordinated and with clear and helpful documentation conveying enthusiasm for the subject.

10 **Good resources** in terms of books, source material, equipment, worksheets, etc.

This book aims to help teachers develop these characteristics of good practice.

'What is different about the revised order?'

1.2 The revised National Curriculum for History

All schools will by now have received and digested their copy of the revised National Curriculum. It includes some significant developments which teachers will need to consider when reviewing their curriculum arrangements for history and planning for the new requirements.

General

There are three main components to the new proposals. These are:

■ **the key elements**, which should be given a prominent place in the planning and delivery of the history study units;

■ **the content of the study units;**

■ **the level descriptions**, which have a much lower status than the old statements of attainment. Their use is largely restricted to reporting at the end of each key stage. There is now just a single attainment target, called 'History'.

Key Stage 1

In Key Stage 1 there are few changes. However:

■ the time periods have been reduced from three to two;

■ the reference to myths, legends and fictional stories has been removed.

In implementing the new proposals, the main concern in many schools will be how to ensure that pupils' experiences of history are not limited solely to the familiar and the local, but that opportunities are found to go beyond this.

Key Stage 1 now includes **key elements** which must be addressed. Therefore, whilst there is still the necessary flexibility in Key Stage 1, teachers will need to check their coverage of the key elements and to ensure that proper attention is given to these skills and ideas, which are associated with the teaching of history in the other key stages.

Key Stage 2

Key Stage 2 is still structured around **study units**, although the amount of content has seemingly been reduced. There are now only six units.

The main changes in content are:

■ the elimination of Explorations and Encounters (although the Aztecs can still be studied as a non-European unit);

■ the removal of the Stuarts from the Tudor and Stuart unit;

■ the elimination of the long-term development study.

Schools should still look at the **focus statements** at the start of each unit to guide planning and coverage of the unit. However, it is important to remember that the planning should not just be based on these study units. The **key elements** must also be seriously addressed across the key stage. This means, amongst other things, that history should be studied from a range of perspectives, including the political, economic, scientific, technological, social, religious, cultural and aesthetic – although there is no longer any requirement to deal substantially with each.

The key elements also require that teaching

■ considers the roles of **women as well as men**;

■ reflects the social, cultural, religious and ethnic **diversity of society**;

■ explores the **range of attitudes**, **ideas and beliefs** of the time.

Schools might have taught in this way before but the significance of these factors is now highlighted.

The key elements have also highlighted the need to make **links and connections** between study units rather than treating history as a series of unconnected episodes. Considering threads which connect different study units will now be necessary. This will present a real challenge to many teachers, as study units are seldom taught in a fixed order in primary schools.

The new order requires that **some aspects of history be tackled in outline, some in depth**. Whilst tackling studies in depth has always been relatively easy, tackling outlines or overviews in an interesting way has been much more difficult. Amongst other things, an outline or overview requires teachers to highlight the key ideas and key questions associated with each unit – a difficult task for non-specialists in particular. Section 2 of this book provides comprehensive help on this matter for each unit.

The attainment target

Although the attainment targets have been integrated into one in the new order, the elements encompassed by them remain largely intact in the key elements and the level descriptions. These are:

■ **knowledge**;

■ an understanding of **chronology**, **time**, **change** and development;

■ explanations for historical actions and developments, including **causation and motivation**;

■ **interpretations**, representations and depictions of history – pupils' awareness that there is more than one way of looking at historical events and issues;

■ **sources** – understanding that history relies on sources of information and that these have to be handled carefully;

■ the **historical process** – encouraging pupils to carry out their own investigations by posing their own questions or hypotheses and locating, organising, questioning and communicating their sources of information.

Historical terms

In addition to the defined content, the key elements list a range of terms which should be taught in Key Stage 2. Teachers need to think how and where they will introduce these terms to pupils.

This book aims to show how these distinctive requirements of the revised Order can be incorporated into history curriculum planning.

'Was the introduction of National Curriculum History a success or a failure?'

1.3 An audit of the early years of National Curriculum History

In this chapter we present our own audit of the first few years of National Curriculum History. What we find is that there is plentiful evidence that National Curriculum History introduced many excellent developments into primary history teaching, while also introducing some problems which have yet to be solved.

Strengths and achievements: ... the pupils' view

These are some of the responses we received when we asked pupils in our own schools what they like about history:

■ *'I like it when we have visitors. We had two visitors who told us what life was like in this school years ago – that was interesting.' (Y2)*

■ *'We visited the Viking museum. I like visits to places.' (Y3)*

■ *'You weren't there when it happened, so it's exciting finding out.' (Y4)*

■ *'It's interesting learning about how other people have lived, other people's lives.' (Y5)*

■ *'I like learning facts about the past that you can tell your children when you are grown up. I also like learning about the way people used to live by dressing up and acting it out. You know what it felt like then.' (Y5)*

■ *'When I was little I used to think about my dad, "How does he know that?" Now I know it myself.' (Y5)*

■ *'Yes, I like telling my parents things they did not know. I say to my dad, "Did you know . . ." and he says, "No, but I expect you are going to tell me." So I do.' (Y6)*

■ *'I like learning about how different people are, about the changes there have been. For example, the Ancient Egyptians learnt about so many things, making paper, ordering time and building pyramids in the deserts, things we know about but they had to learn.' (Y6)*

... the teachers' view

These are some of the responses we received when we asked colleagues what they thought were the successes of National Curriculum History:

- *'Before the National Curriculum, we used to look down on history. Like its content, it was an age that had gone. To teach it was old-fashioned. Now we have to teach it, we are glad it's in the curriculum.'* (KS2 teacher)

- *'History-led topics in this school always go down well.'* (KS2 teacher)

- *'Pupils do not seem to tire of finding out about the local history topic. They bring in many objects and information from home. Parents talk to me about the topic at the school open day.'* (KS1 teacher)

- *'I wish I knew more about the topics. I do not know enough to make some of the topics really interesting. If I had a year off I would spend much of it researching more history. It's got me hooked.'* (KS2 teacher)

- *'I was not the only one to say that history was totally unsuitable for my young pupils. How wrong I was. The only place where I was right was in remembering facts and dates. Once we learnt that this was not really what National Curriculum History was about, I and the class always enjoyed the history.'* (KS1 teacher)

- *'Probably the most successful of the National Curriculum subjects in our school. If only we could make geography as successful.'* (KS2 teacher)

- *'Even Ancient Egypt and Greece have gone down well.'* (KS2 teacher)

... the inspectors' view

The comments of advisers and inspectors confirm that the History National Curriculum has brought many positive developments to schools.

These developments provide a strong foundation to build on in the future and OFSTED has summarised them as follows:

HISTORY IS AN ESTABLISHED PART OF THE CURRICULUM

History has gained what OFSTED calls a 'significant and accepted place' in the primary curriculum.

- There is a great deal of history going on.

- The displays of historical work are prominent in many schools.

- Many topics in primary schools have a history focus and recognisable history is apparent.

- Many teachers view history positively.

- Pupils often speak with enthusiasm about the history they have covered.

- More money was spent by schools on resourcing history than had been the case before the days of the National Curriculum.

HISTORY IS USUALLY BEING WELL TAUGHT

Inspectors looking at the **quality of teaching and learning** in primary schools paint a satisfactory and improving picture, especially in Key Stage 1.

Their 1992–93 report noted how standards were satisfactory or better in 80 per cent of Key Stage 1 lessons and 70 per cent of Key Stage 2 lessons. OFSTED reported enthusiastically about skills of sequencing, chronological understanding and confidence in handling sources.

What makes this particularly pleasing is to compare these comments with the inspectors' assessment that there was poor-quality history work in many primary schools prior to the National Curriculum.

PUPILS HAVE A RANGE OF LEARNING EXPERIENCES

The **variety of pupil experiences of history** has been extended.

■ Fears expressed about declining numbers of school visits caused by charging policies and time pressures have not applied to all schools. Inspectors and others have praised the use of resources outside the classroom.

■ Artefacts have been well used in schools, especially in Key Stage 1. Some schools still have access to loan collections and many more are supplemented by the ingenuity of teachers and the goodwill of parents.

■ Many primary schools have also drawn on the experience of others. They have brought in older people from their community and local experts such as archaeologists, archivists and museum curators. In some schools local craftspeople and musicians have enhanced the teaching of the history of a topic or period.

HISTORY HAS BEEN WELL INTEGRATED INTO THE CURRICULUM

Although history tends to be a distinctive subject, it has been **integrated well into whole-curriculum planning and harnessed effectively to the teaching of other curriculum areas**. For example:

■ Archaeology has been harnessed to science teaching.

■ Language work and history have become closely intertwined.

■ Technology and geography have been combined with history, sometimes very successfully.

■ Schools have seen the value of information technology, not just for word processing but for computer-aided design and data handling – for example, using a computer to analyse local census data as part of local history.

■ Links have been developed between music and history.

■ The critical appraisal of visual images has combined art and history.

THE HISTORY CURRICULUM HAS BEEN COHERENTLY PLANNED

Pre-National Curriculum, much history was a 'lucky dip', with very little thought given to coherence or progression. **Planning has improved considerably** even if it is not yet perfect.

Many schools have produced frameworks which delineate how history is to be covered through Key Stages 1 and 2. They have also devised policies and schemes of work to provide much firmer guidance on teaching the subject.

MANAGEMENT OF THE HISTORY CURRICULUM HAS IMPROVED

Schools have also **improved their management and organisation of the subject**. Many schools now have history coordinators. This has not been easy and the role of the coordinator is still being defined in some schools.

There are particular problems in small schools where there are too many subjects and too few teachers to allow expertise to develop effectively.

TEACHERS' PROFESSIONAL DEVELOPMENT HAS CONTINUED

Teacher expertise is developing, although there is still a long way to go. Current teacher training gives a more prominent place to the subject for non-specialists.

Problems and concerns: ... the pupils' view

Despite the good points noted above, all is not yet well.

When we asked the same pupils what they dislike about history, these were some of the responses they made:

- *'It's interesting but I do not know when I will ever need the information.' (Y6)*

- *'I never seem to be able to remember what I have learnt.' (Y3)*

- *'There are some good stories but I am not sure if many of them are true. I prefer stories about spacemen.' (Y4)*

- *'My mum and dad are fed up with me pestering them about what they used to live like when they were little.' (Y4)*

- *'I like it now but my sister says that it gets boring when you get older.' (Y4)*

- *'It's hard work especially when we write.' (Y6)*

... the teachers' view

Teachers up and down the country also report a wide range of worries about the early years of the National Curriculum. For example:

- *'There's not enough time to cover all the content.'*

- *'I'm not an expert. I'm really only one step ahead of the pupils.'*

- *'It's impossible to organise history successfully in a small school like mine.'*

- *'To be honest I only pay lip-service to assessment in history.'*

- *'I've bought lots of nice resources but I'm not getting the best out of them.'*

- *'In a middle school organising coverage of the units is a nightmare.'*

- *'I never liked history – I'm still not sure it's very relevant to my kids.'*

- *'The big problem is cross-curricular planning.'*

- *'It's still male, English, white history. It's not suitable for our children.'*

- *'I'm not sure I know what good history from my pupils is .'*

Some of these views are commonly heard. Many of them have been important considerations in the reviewing of the National Curriculum.

... the inspectors' view

WHERE IS THE 'TOTAL HISTORY EXPERIENCE'?

OFSTED has expressed two linked worries about National Curriculum History.

Although pupils are receiving aspects of a historical education, in many schools they are not getting a total history experience. This is apparent in two areas:

1   **The historical process:** Good history is a careful mix of knowledge and process. Much history teaching, especially in Key Stage 2, covers content well but is less effective in engaging the pupils in the historical process.

When historians talk about the historical process, they mean carrying out a historical investigation, which involves pupils in the following tasks:

■   posing questions to investigate;

■   thinking about the sources of information to use;

■   locating them;

■   interpreting and questioning them;

■   recording and organising information;

■   reaching conclusions;

■   communicating the conclusions in a logical, interesting and relevant manner.

While it is clearly not practical for pupils to approach all historical content using this process, there is no reason why primary pupils should not use it, with appropriate teacher support, for some units, especially for those aspects studied in depth.

It is all too easy to underestimate what pupils are capable of. As pupils progress through Key Stages 1 and 2, one clear sign of progression should be their ability to carry out these various aspects of the historical process. We deal with this in greater detail in Section 2.

Some areas in which pupils' historical skills are not being sufficiently developed in many schools are:

■   Activities often go no further than extracting information from topic books or observational drawing.

■   Even where a more ambitious and time-consuming approach is used – e.g. looking at a picture of a Viking ship and then making a model of one – the product is seen as an end in itself and is rarely used to develop pupils' historical understanding.

■   Few primary schools have used sources in ways that go much further than observation and comprehension.

■   Likewise, visits to historical sites go no further than filling in worksheets to test drawing and observational skills.

■   Displays sometimes consist of little more than published posters.

There are obviously encouraging instances of pupils devising and carrying out their own historical enquiry – having the chance to show that they are capable of real historical thinking – but they rarely have this opportunity in many schools.

2 **The diversity of society:** In many schools there has been little attempt to reflect the social, cultural, religious and ethnic diversity of the society being studied. Likewise, there has been little attempt to address the role of women as well as men.

THE STRUCTURE OF THE NATIONAL CURRICULUM HAS BEEN A HINDRANCE

The structure of the National Curriculum has been partly to blame for this failing. The content-defined study unit has been handy as a planning device for primary teachers but the study units never made explicit the skills and concepts that needed to be used and developed. The emphasis was predominantly on content.

Furthermore, the general requirements which carried important messages about the historical process and about the need to reflect the diversity of society and to look at history from a range of perspectives, were tucked away at the front of the document and were widely ignored.

In the new order the gathering together of such requirements in the key elements should ensure that they become much more prominent in future planning.

Planning a primary history curriculum

'What is a "total history experience", and how can I make sure our children have it?'

2.1 A total history experience

One way of summing up the main criticism of the implementation of National Curriculum History so far is that pupils are not given a 'total' experience of history. Pupils cover the content, they encounter stories – and even evidence – from the past, but they are not taken through the process of investigation that is at the heart of history. They end up 'doing' yet another period of history but they don't progress in their historical skills and understanding.

We hope to show that this need not be the case. Historical content can be investigated by pupils in a stimulating way so that they *do* develop their historical skills and understanding. The examples in this section are designed to show how this may be done.

To start with, however, there are a number of principles to bear in mind:

■ **The content listed in the study units does not all need to be treated in equal detail.** The 'focus' statement at the top of each unit suggests where you might put the emphasis. You might alternatively wish to focus on a different aspect of the unit. Whichever path you choose, it is essential to remember that some parts of the content will need to be covered in outline and other parts in detail. Planning needs to allow for both approaches.

■ **The content can be viewed from a variety of perspectives.** The key elements in the new Order still require consideration of a number of historical perspectives – political, economic, scientific, technological, social, religious, cultural and aesthetic – although it is no longer a rigid requirement to cover all of them in each unit. Viewing content from different and surprising perspectives can set up much more creative possibilities for planning a history programme.

■ **Content can be used in a variety of ways.** The key elements provide a variety of ways of looking at historical content. Some content is ideal for improving pupils' sense of chronology or their understanding of causes and results; some is ideal for developing their sense of the social, cultural, religious and ethnic diversity or of the role played by women in society; other content is ideal for helping pupils become familiar with the range of historical terms which they need for each key stage.

It is important that the approaches to history implied by the key elements are a major part of your planning for pupils' historical learning. The following examples show one school's approach to planning for distinct areas of the key elements in Key Stages 1 and 2 (chronology and change – 1a and 1b; reasons and results – 2b; interpretations – 3a; historical investigation – 4a, 4b and 5c).

Chronology and change (Key Elements 1a and 1b)

As pupils progress they will increasingly realise:

■ **that all people, events and objects did not live, happen or exist simultaneously and that some are older than others.** This is a barrier that needs to be broken down early on. Pupils should try to understand that a world existed before they or those around them were born. As they progress they may see that human time is only a small part of total time and that the past is connected to the present.

■ **that we use conventions to describe time and duration.** In the earliest stages they can use familiar conventions, such as days of the week and years, and gradually move to more complex terms such as century, generation and period labels such as Roman or Tudor.

■ **that some things change over time.** Early on they need to see that the past was different in many aspects, and they will extend their ability to detect similarities and differences.

■ **that some things change more rapidly than others.** As they progress they should see that things change and that some have changed very slowly, others more rapidly and some not at all. They should realise that old and new things can exist alongside each other. They may point out that some things have changed in part but not totally.

■ **that there are different kinds of change.** They will increasingly recognise different kinds of change: e.g. slow, rapid, unimportant, important, 'good' and 'bad' changes and developments. They may begin to recognise that change can be good for some and bad for others. They may be able to use the word 'progress' appropriately.

■ **changes are connected so that one change can lead to another.** At the end of Key Stage 2, pupils may be able to see that a change can affect all sorts of things and can be responsible for producing other changes. At the highest levels pupils will see that there are often several reasons for change and it is rarely caused by just one person's actions.

EXAMPLE 2.1: CHRONOLOGY AND CHANGE

A sense of chronology and the concept of the passing of time are essential to historical thinking, so a variety of activities are needed to develop pupils' skills.

Sequencing and timeline activities are already common in both Key Stages 1 and 2. Activities have been devised which address both history and maths objectives with regard to describing and understanding time.

The school in the following example had two Key Stage 1 topics in which there were good opportunities for developing a sense of chronology and change – 'People I Know' and 'Ourselves and our Families'.

The teachers recognised some of the problems of teaching time and chronology to younger pupils. For example, five-year-olds can rarely use numbers beyond 100; they have little sense of relative duration or of passing time. Research (by Crowther and others – see select Bibliography) suggests that even seven-year-olds see change in terms of someone substituting one thing for another. Only in Key Stage 2 is there likely to be a gradual recognition of succession and continuity.

Given these constraints, the school devised a range of activities to improve pupils' understanding of chronology and change, including the following:

1 Children were asked to identify the differences between babies and five-year-old children through the use of photographs of themselves as babies and up-to-date photographs. Pictorial lists of what babies and five-year-olds can do were produced and displayed under the headings: 'What I could do as a baby' and

What I can do now'. Children then moved on to a sorting activity in which they placed photographs of babies and children of their own age whom they knew into the categories 'now' and 'then', i.e. what Katie looked like then and what Katie looks like now.

2 Children were asked to bring photographs of themselves aged one, two, three, four and five and to sort them into the right sequence. They could then select from a range of objects or pictures the most appropriate one to match the age of the child in each photograph, e.g. walk-along toy, school uniform, birthday card with age on it, photograph of birthday cake. Pupils were then asked to sequence a wider range of ages from babies to elderly people. Various objects and pictures were provided and pupils had to match these to the various ages.

3 Pupils were asked to sequence a number of different artefacts. Some used toys, some buildings, some types of heating and others types of lighting. At the age of seven pupils can cope with four or five objects.

The 'lighting' example in Figures 2.1 – 2.3 was done by a class of five- and six-year-olds. Pupils had to describe and draw the object, place it in one of two categories ('a long time ago' and 'now') and state what they thought the object was used for and why they had put it into the category.

This activity revealed and challenged some of the pupils' preconceptions, e.g. that things which are broken, dirty, smaller, rusty, black and white etc. are invariably older.

If the activity was being done with seven-year-olds, they might be able to use more categories, e.g. 'oldest', 'middle' and 'youngest/newest'.

4 Children identified aspects of their lives that had changed over time and aspects that had remained the same. They were helped to understand why this was the case: for example, they moved house because their existing house was too small or because a parent had changed jobs.

Figures 2.1 and 2.2

Rebecca

The Oil Lamp   Bicycle Light

A Long time ago   Now

I think it is old   I do think it is New
because it is rusty.   because it's got 2 batterles.
I think it was used   It is used on a bicycle.
in the coal mine   It works by electricity
It used oil to work.

✓

Well tried ✓
Rebecca.

Figure 2.3

5 Key Stage 1 children asked Key Stage 2 children (Year 6) about their memories of being five years old. The older children brought in and described games and toys they had, clothes they wore, television programmes they watched. They considered similarities and differences between their lives and the lives of the older children at the age of five. Photos of the older children at the age of five were added to class timelines in appropriate positions.

6 The idea of generations was introduced to pupils. Pupils talked to parents and familiar adults about their memories of being five years old. Simple family trees with photos of the family members showed the relationships of the generations to each other, although specific time spans were avoided in the early years.

7 Pupils were introduced to some of the ways of telling the time now and in the past, e.g. candle and water clocks, sundials, modern clocks and watches, calendars.

8 A list of time terms was established and opportunities were taken to introduce, use and reinforce the terms: long ago, once upon a time, new, old, young, then, now, before, after, today, morning, afternoon, yesterday, tomorrow, second, minute, hour, days of the week, seasons, months.

9 Pupils had boxes which were assigned to a given individual in history. They had to place in the box objects that that person might have had.

10 Pupils produced timelines of their own lives and the lives of members of their immediate family, noting significant events such as birthdays and starting school.

Early timelines should go backwards from the present. Sequence rather than scale is important with the youngest pupils. Years and decades can be scaled by Year 2.

Each class also had large timelines (made of a washing line and pegs) at a suitable height for historical sources, photos of artefacts, pictures and quotations to be added to it. They took care, however, not to clutter the timeline so that the main shape of the period was obscured.

Reasons and results (Key Element 2b)

As pupils progress they will increasingly realise:

■ **that events happen for a reason.** Pupils need to grasp at an early stage that things do not just happen. To start with they will think in terms of people making things happen. Increasingly they will realise that other reasons may lead to something happening.

■ **that people can change things in a variety of ways.** Pupils will increasingly understand that people's actions can have unexpected or unintended results, and that these can be good or bad. They will see that people in the past were not one amorphous mass, all thinking and acting the same way. They will see how the differences in their situation might have affected the choices they made or the actions they took.

■ **that causes and results are connected.** As they progress, pupils will become better at finding the connections between reasons and results. They will increasingly see that a number of results can stem from a particular cause or event. However, this is a high-level skill so they may find it difficult.

■ **that there are different types of causes and results.** At first they are likely to recognise single causes (e.g. a named individual caused a particular event to happen). As they progress they will see a fuller range of causes or results and even make judgements, for example which were more important, which took a long time to happen, and which happened suddenly. They may also realise at the highest levels that the importance of an event is not necessarily connected to the number of causes or consequences it has.

■ **that causes are connected to each other.** At first pupils may simply see the reasons for an event as everything that happened before the event. As they progress they may learn to distinguish the causes of the event from all the precursors. They may comment that a given event might not have happened if something else had not happened or someone had acted differently. Eventually they may be able to grasp that some causes were connected to each other.

■ **that it is not always possible to know why events occurred and why people acted as they did.** As pupils become familiar with the way history is constructed they will start to understand that it does not provide all the answers. They will realise that the sources are too limited and that we can only guess at some of the answers. However, as they progress, the quality of their conjecture will improve so that it becomes more than a guess.

EXAMPLE 2.2: REASONS AND RESULTS

A Key Stage 1 teacher in a small primary school was keen to develop a basic understanding of reasons and results in her class of Year 1 and Year 2 pupils.

She was acutely aware that published resources provided a lot of work on change but a lot less on causation and motivation. She knew that research into the competencies of children tended to be pessimistic about young pupils' understanding of reasons and results. Knight, for example (see Select Bibliography), sees this ability really taking off between the ages of seven and nine.

The teacher of the Year 1/2 class also served as the school's history consultant. She felt that pupils both could and should have some awareness of causation in Key Stage 1. She was aware of the need to strike a careful balance between the gains to be had from focusing specifically on developing the key ideas associated with reasons and results, and the problems of doing something that did not integrate effectively with the programme of study.

It was decided that the topic entitled 'Ourselves and Our Families' would have a particular but not exclusive emphasis on causation. The aim was to use natural but frequent opportunities to develop an understanding of the concept. The main intention was constantly to use the two words 'why' and 'because' in a range of contexts so that the ideas would be reinforced.

The plan was not too ambitious. The work would be as personal as possible.

The following are some of the activities that were introduced to foster an understanding of reasons and results.

1 Pupils were asked to think of occasions when they had been happy, sad and excited. They drew pictures of themselves in these situations. They then had to think of one reason why they had experienced each of these feelings. These reasons were written on a piece of card either by the pupils or with the teacher's help. Pupils then matched their explanations to the pictures. At first the pupils found this easy – just matching three reasons to three pictures. The teacher then added two or three more descriptions which were invented causes. Pupils had to isolate the real causes. They then worked in pairs, trying to do the same for their partner's three pictures.

2 Pupils discussed some of the things they did or that happened to them at different times of the year, e.g. in winter and summer, at Christmas, on November 5, on Diwali. For every event they referred to, they were asked to think why it happened at that particular time.

The teacher tried to encourage pupils to consider whether there was more than one reason for an event happening, e.g. for summer holidays they came up with the fact that there were breaks away from school and that the weather was better. In most cases, however, the pupils found it difficult to suggest more than one reason for an event.

3 The grandmother of one of the pupils came in to talk to pupils about her family life during the Second World War. She was well prepared.

Prior to her visit pupils had worked in groups to prepare questions, most of which specifically asked why things had happened. Pupils wrote the questions on one side of a large piece of paper.

The session with the grandparent was taped. By listening to the tape they were able to find relevant answers to the questions.

To reinforce understanding the original questions were then covered over, leaving only the answers visible. Pupils had to recall or work out what the original question had been.

4 Pupils listened to a story about a poor family in Victorian times which involved child labour in a cotton mill and a later period when the whole family had had to go into the workhouse. At the end of the story pupils spent some time talking about the events and why they had happened.

In small groups, the pupils were then given a series of picture cards depicting some of the events in the story. The first task was to sequence the cards to reconstruct the story. The teacher then gave out a number of cards listing the reasons for the events shown on each of the sequence cards. Pupils had to try to match them up.

A later activity involved pupils trying to work out what events in the story would not happen to a family alive today and to say why this was so.

5 The teacher told a true story of a family evacuated to the neighbourhood of the school. The teacher told three-quarters of the story, stopping at a critical point when various results might be likely to follow. Pupils then had to draw or role play what they thought the ending would be and explain why they had come to this conclusion. Endings varied. The teacher then gave the true ending. One purpose of this exercise was to show that results are not always expected or predictable.

The activity also involved pupils being given a series of cards with drawings. They included aeroplanes, bombs, children being evacuated by train, a picture of evacuated children in the countryside and a bombed city. Pupils then had to separate pictures which showed reasons for evacuation from those which showed results. This last exercise was possible only for the more able Year 2 pupils.

6 The teacher used every occasion to ask a series of reasons/results questions throughout the topic. These included:

- Why did a person make a particular decision?

- Why did people like or dislike doing something?

- Why had something changed?

- How and why had some object improved?

- Why do we do things differently to how parents and grandparents might have done them?

- Why do pupils think something about the past is true or false?

- Were pupils surprised at the ending of a particular historical story?

- How did people feel about particular situations in historical stories, e.g. angry, anxious, happy?

Interpretations and representations (Key Element 3a)

As pupils progress they will increasingly see:

- **that people put their own ideas into history.** Pupils need to be introduced early on to the fact that there is nearly always more than one way of looking at an event or person. Through the primary years children should increasingly realise that history is not 'out there' waiting to be recorded but that people make history – history is constructed by different people in different ways. This is a difficult idea but it can be approached at a basic level by pointing out that the people who write history books, make history television programmes or lead guided tours of museums or stately homes put their own ideas into what they say. Different people can therefore give different impressions of a period, a place or an event.

- **that disagreements and differences in versions of history do not mean that one is right and the other is wrong.** At first pupils will assume that all accounts of the past are true, and later that if there are differences one version must be wrong. Older pupils, however, will start to see that some accounts of the past are more trustworthy than others: e.g. one may use more reliable sources of information, or take greater care. It may be possible for more able pupils to grasp that differences can arise for quite valid reasons, e.g. historians having different beliefs or different agendas, and so one account is not necessarily better than another.

- **that history cannot cover everything, so some kind of selection is needed.** Pupils will, with experience, understand that we cannot know everything there is to know about the past, still less put it down in writing. What follows is that history is necessarily selective and that what we select to write about is our interpretation of the past.

EXAMPLE 2.3: INTERPRETATIONS

A Key Stage 1 teacher was initially pessimistic about pupils' ability to cope with different representations and interpretations. Her experience led her to believe that Year 1 and 2 pupils find differing viewpoints confusing and that they like certainty. She also felt that a real grasp of different interpretations required detailed historical knowledge which was lacking in pupils of that age range.

However, she decided to try to deal with some of the relevant issues when teaching a topic entitled 'Children and Animals'. Below is her assessment of some of the strategies used.

'I was advised against trying to be too ambitious; better to use a range of approaches to get over the idea to most of the pupils that there are often two ways of looking at things. I decided to do this through contrasting stories.

1　I wanted the interpretations to come as much as possible from the pupils themselves. I felt that if the different interpretations came from them rather than from external sources, then they stood a better chance of understanding things. So I began by telling them a story. Since the topic was 'Children and Animals', I based it loosely on a Beatrix Potter story.

After I had finished, I asked them to think of something that may have happened after the end of the story. We then went over some of those new endings. I asked them which was the right ending. Although a few pupils thought there was a definite 'right' ending, others realised that there could not be any right one. Even so, many believed that the most satisfying ending was the correct one.

2　I then moved on to a history story. It was one I had made up myself about a family living in London during the Blitz. The story told of shelters, fear, bombs, spending time underground, and evacuation. I then gave pupils a series of sequence cards re-telling the story which they had to organise. However, I did not have cards of all the story and I told them that there was one card missing. Each child had to draw his or her own sequence card of the missing part of the story. The pupils then compared their drawings of the 'missing' event. As expected (and hoped for), a variety of events was depicted. Several pupils now began to understand that, although the drawings showed different aspects, they were all correct in their own way.

3　I prepared two stories about children going to school in Victorian times. One version of the story was written from the point of view of someone who loved school, clearly liked the teachers and lessons, and described the facilities with affection. The other was a story about someone who was badly behaved and disliked school intensely.

Whilst the Year 2 pupils were elsewhere, I told the Year 1 pupils the story of the child who enjoyed school. I also gave out a worksheet I had prepared with some pictures and information about the school.

I then told the Year 2 children, who were at this time in the classroom on their own, the story representing the other viewpoint – again accompanying it with an information sheet.

Pupils then worked in pairs to prepare a brief account of what their Victorian person felt about school. Once this was done, a Year 1 pair swapped their brief account with a Year 2 pair. They were asked to note similarities and differences.

Most recognised these easily. It was also gratifying to see that many children recognised that the two versions could be based on the same school but could represent different attitudes. Some even tried to explain the different views by relating them to standards of academic success or behaviour. However, there were still a few children who thought one of the versions was wrong.

4　I had become aware that one of the most difficult areas of the original statements of attainment for young pupils was the requirement to distinguish fact from fantasy. However, I wanted to get over the idea that some of the things they read in stories were true and others false.

We devised a series of stories about animals and people. At first, many pupils made a clear distinction: the stories about people were true, whereas those about animals – especially talking animals and those living in houses and wearing clothes – were not.

I gradually made things more difficult by focusing largely on stories about people, telling pupil's that some of the people were real and others were not. Some were straightforward, such as stories about people they knew to be real, e.g. teachers and people who had visited the school. The problem occurred with people who could have been real but who appeared in stories in obviously unreal situations, e.g. Little Red Riding Hood.

I was surprised how confused some of the pupils were. Nevertheless, the discussion about some of the characters and the reasons they gave for their answers made the exercise worthwhile. I was also able to reinforce the terms 'real people' and 'fiction'.

5 I wanted to reinforce the idea of different people seeing the same event from different angles.

In part, we did this by using a class story, Judy Blume's *The Pain and the Great One*, in which part of the story is told from the viewpoint of an older sister or brother.

We also took a character from history – Henry VIII. I told a story about Henry which depicted his bravery; another teacher told a brief story about his cruelty. We used a clip from the film *Henry VIII and his Six Wives*, as well as one or two pictures. When the pupils had been given four different depictions, they were asked to draw a picture showing Henry VIII 'in action' and put a caption underneath. We then discussed the different versions. Some of the Year 2 pupils were able to offer some reasons for the differences between these interpretations.

6 Finally, pupils were asked to think of six objects they might choose to put in a time capsule so that anyone finding it in the future (pupils often seem to understand the concept of the future better than the concept of the past) would be able to work out what a child's life was like now. Once the pupils had made their lists, these were compared. By now pupils seemed to understand that there was not necessarily one 'right' answer for such tasks. Throughout the activities I tried to encourage them to use words such as 'probably', 'may be' and 'could be'.

EXAMPLE 2.4: INTERPRETATIONS

One Key Stage 2 school used a field trip to Lincoln Castle to develop work on interpretations. The children were thinking about Victorian crime and punishment – for many years, Lincoln Castle had served as a court-house, prison and place of execution.

When the pupils were looking around the castle, they were directed towards a series of gravestones and to one in particular, that of Pricilla Bickerdyke. Bickerdyke was accused and convicted of murdering her husband and subsequently hanged at Lincoln prison in the 19th century. The details are well documented and pupils were set the task of preparing, in groups, a re-enactment of the trial based on the evidence.

Using published local history books, broadsides and transcripts of records of the trial, as well as a range of source material and topic books about Victorian crime and attitudes to crime, the Year 6 pupils were divided into two groups to prepare the prosecution and defence cases. Prior to this, the teacher had given some explanation of the way that criminal trials operate. Pupils were allowed some time to prepare their case.

The aim was a role play of the trial with pupils from Year 5 – who knew nothing about the outcome but who had done some work on Victorian times – acting as the jury.

The trial was a great success. Scenes from the trial, as well as of pupils' preparation, can be seen in the photographs in Figures 2.4 – 2.7. Such was the spirit with which pupils joined in, that when the verdict was announced the girl playing Pricilla Bickerdyke fainted. In addition to photographic evidence, the teacher took a video of the trial to allow for follow-up work.

The Year 5 jury found Bickerdyke not guilty, while the real trial found her guilty. The teacher used this opportunity to develop pupils' understanding of the concept of interpretations.

1 Pupils who had prepared the defence and prosecution cases showed how their arguments depended on the selective use of evidence. The teacher specifically used the slants of the two cases to show that a historian or writer could make people think in a particular way, not by telling lies but simply by what they chose to include and what they chose to leave out of their account.

2 The teacher wanted to convey the idea that the way in which somebody interprets a historical event depends partly on the source material used and partly on how the reader views that material. Considerable

Figure 2.4

Figure 2.5

Figure 2.6

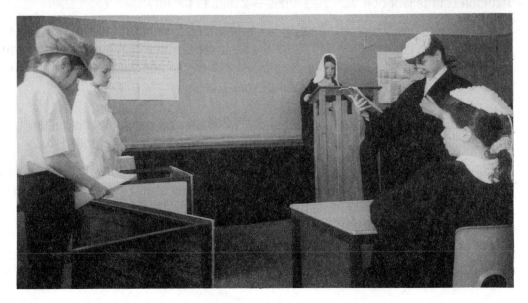

Figure 2.7

attention was paid to the nature of the source material presented. Pupils on both the defence and prosecution sides were constantly challenged by the teacher to consider whether different source material could have strengthened or weakened their case. The Year 5 jurors were also quizzed as to whether they felt the evidence was sufficient or convincing enough to sustain the case.

3 The other message the teacher wanted to convey was that interpretations are often 'in the eye of the beholder'. She pointed out that a Victorian jury had heard similar evidence. The facts had been quite similar but the verdicts had been different. Some of the more able Year 6 pupils could see that the way something is both presented and received is influenced by the audience and their beliefs and values.

To follow up the discussions arising from the trial, the teacher tried a number of different strategies to reinforce the idea that history is represented and interpreted in different ways by different people for different reasons.

4 She introduced as many different forms of representation of the Victorian period as possible. Whenever a new representation was used for the first time, she asked a range of questions about the way in which the period, or a character within it, had been depicted. Pupils were regularly asked to consider how and why something had been represented in the way it was. Amongst the sources used were film clips, fiction such as Dickens novels, poems, an IT simulation, a local display in the Lincolnshire Life Museum, a song and even a television advert depicting Victorian life. Use was also made of a range of topic books, including some older school textbooks, as well as the County Library Loan topic collections.

5 Pupils were given selected evidence about various aspects of Victorian life, including education and working conditions. Pupils produced accounts based on the evidence. Different versions were then compared.

6 Small groups of pupils had to plan a museum display about Victorian Britain. They had to produce diagrams and an explanation of what they would include to represent the Victorian period and how they would lay it out. They also used IT to produce some sample captions.

The different representations were then compared, with groups explaining why they thought their version represented Victorian Britain. Although there was no time to arrange a school visit, pupils were encouraged to visit the local museums with their parents at weekends to compare their versions with the professional displays.

7 Pupils were given a series of brief paragraphs referring to aspects of Victorian Britain. The task was to work out questions that might have led to such responses. The purpose behind this was to increase understanding of the fact that the way in which history is written is dependent on the questions asked.

8 Small groups of pupils were asked to write a brief account of an event in a way which they felt would reflect the viewpoint of a particular reader in Victorian times, e.g. the Queen, a mill owner, a factory worker. They were partly directed to specific sources including those in the school library.

In conjunction with this, pupils were introduced to words such as 'bias' and 'opinion'. Pupils finishing this task quickly were asked to amend their version to reflect a different interest.

Some pupils found the written work difficult. To help them, the teacher had prepared on the computer some distorted versions reflecting a particular view. These pupils then had to use the 'delete' or 'bold' facility to remove or highlight the phrases which were responsible for producing the distortions.

A few pupils were also asked to produce a drawing reflecting a particular viewpoint.

Historical investigation (Key Elements 4a, 4b and 5c)

As pupils progress they will increasingly be able:

■ **to devise their own questions to investigate.** At the most basic level this will involve pupils saying what they would like to find out about a particular period. As they progress they can begin to identify certain questions as being more appropriate for investigation than others.

■ **to use, interpret and critically evaluate sources.** The base line for pupils progressing in this area is their understanding that people in the past left evidence of their existence and activities, and that this evidence is what we use to pursue our investigations. However, pupils increasingly realise that for some periods no evidence survives – although they should also begin to appreciate, perhaps through practice, that too much source material can cause problems as well as too little. They will realise, again through practice, that getting answers to their questions from sources is not like mining coal from a seam. Many sources are problematic; they contain conflicting information, inaccuracy, distortion. Pupils will gradually start to realise that they need to ask questions about the sources and that critical evaluation is a key part of history work. As pupils progress, they will work out ways of checking the sources and of understanding problems using a range of sources.

■ **to provide clear, convincing and uncluttered information;**

■ **to make valid inferences;**

■ **to explain as well as describe;**

■ **to choose the best ways to communicate their work;**

■ **to understand the tentative nature of their work.** As a pupil's grasp of the historical process increases, his or her own responses should recognise the uncertainty of history. In many respects, the most immature approach to history is an unquestioning one. Pupils should become aware of the problems of doing history and the role of their own prejudices and preferences.

EXAMPLE 2.5: THE HISTORICAL PROCESS

A small primary school which taught reception, Year 1 and Year 2 pupils within the same classroom aimed to introduce pupils to various aspects of the historical process including source-based work. The topic plans put a particular emphasis on 'doing' history in the topic on 'Homes'.

Various objectives were set. These included:

■ to get pupils to use a range of different types of source material including artefacts, buildings and sites, pictures and photographs, and some source extracts;

■ to encourage pupils to use source material to answer specific questions;

■ to develop pupils' skills in posing as well as answering simple historical questions;

■ to develop pupils' ability to communicate their findings in an appropriate way;

■ to increase historical knowledge and improve understanding of concepts such as causation, change and sequence.

The key activities were as follows:

1 Pupils spent some time discussing pictures of different types of homes. These included large stately homes, caves, igloos, bungalows, tower blocks, Victorian terraces and recent housing. The purpose was twofold: firstly, to ensure that pupils had a working vocabulary – many terms which adults use are not understood by children; secondly, to allow comparison of the features of the different homes. Pupils were then asked to sequence some of the buildings on a timeline.

2 Pupils were introduced to plans of a house. They wrote labels and attached them to the correct rooms. They were then shown a series of artefacts and pictures of a number of objects such as plates, old beds, toys, candlesticks, kitchen items, old chairs and tapestries. They were encouraged to observe the artefacts closely, describing them and considering questions such as what they were made of, their design and what possible use some of them may have had. They then had to decide in which room on the plan the objects belonged. Objects were drawn and the use of scale was encouraged.

3 Pupils were provided with other sources which contained pictures of artefacts and rooms in Victorian houses. Some of these were in commercial topic books but some were from magazines and posters. The task given to pupils was to look for items belonging in houses which they had not already placed on their plan. They were also asked to find out the names of the items. Reference skills using indexes and chapter headings were encouraged.

4 Letters were sent home and pupils were encouraged to bring in household objects which represented different ages. These were discussed in class before being placed on a timeline in the classroom. Discussion took place about the sequence and the use which the objects had. In a few cases pupils were asked to role play a small scene involving the use of one of these objects.

5 A visit was organised to a local museum to see a reconstruction of a Victorian living room. Before they went, pupils were asked to write down what they expected to find in that reconstruction. The museum had been forewarned about the visit. The visit, when it took place, was tightly focused on this display alone. Pupils had thought in advance about questions they wished to ask the curator, e.g. whether it was the room of a rich or poor person, what some of the objects might have been used for, how comfortable they felt the room was. Pupils marked objects on plans and wrote down the names of the objects. When they returned to the classroom, they were asked to add certain objects to their original plans. They were also asked to consider whether some of the items they had included in their original plans ought to be removed because they were not appropriate to a Victorian house, e.g. a television, a Tudor chair.

6 On a sheet of paper, pupils were asked to write about and make drawings to show the similarities and differences between houses in Victorian times and those of today. To help them, they were shown photographs and postcards of Victorian and modern houses. Considerable time was spent developing observational skills with the pictures, e.g. by using a magnifying glass to look for clues.

7 Although some difficulty was experienced, the teacher wanted to introduce pupils to the idea of authenticity. They were shown a replica and told that this had just been made. They were also asked to distinguish pictures from photographs. Other misconceptions were challenged, e.g. that if there are old people in a photograph, it means the photograph is old, and that black and white pictures are older than colour ones. One difficulty was that pupils preferred working from large, clear colour pictures, but many of the pictures from this period were black and white.

8 To conclude the work pupils produced a display collage. This included brief written descriptions of aspects of a Victorian house and what it was like to live there. There were also scale drawings, paintings and a timeline noting some of the features covered in the topic. Since the area surrounding the school contained buildings of different ages and types, a small trail was made with drawings and plans and captions to various features.

9 The home corner for that term involved a Victorian living room. Costumes were obtained to aid authenticity.

EXAMPLE 2.6: HISTORICAL INVESTIGATION

This is an account of work done by pupils in Years 5 and 6 as part of a local history unit which was linked to a study of Victorian Britain. The pupils were already familiar with life in the Victorian countryside through their work on part of the Victorian Times unit. They had carried out a range of activities using topic books, local history materials and television programmes such as *How We Used to Live*.

The aim of the teacher was to involve pupils in various aspects of the historical process. The end product was a story based on the range of sources studied. The story was made up by the children but the intention was that it could have been true in that it conformed with the evidence provided by the sources.

The relevant aims of the activity were:

■ to interrogate and analyse a wide range of original source material including censuses, directories, maps, school records, text and topic books, and the local environment;

■ to work collaboratively by posing and answering questions, making deductions and inferences and organising and communicating in a range of forms including information technology;

■ to improve knowledge and understanding, especially about Victorian England and the pupils' local environment.

The following were the main activities.

1 The teacher did not want to throw the pupils into their research unprepared, so each of the main sources to be used was introduced to all the pupils.

Pupils were shown copies of the original documents as well as transcripts. They were told about the reliability of source material and carried out some exercises to develop skills of observation and interpretation.

The range of sources was considerable and included trade directories; the 1861, 1871 and 1881 censuses; large-scale maps; newspapers; photographs; a range of school records including plans, registers, log books and admission registers; gravestones; a tour of the village comparing 19th-century features with those of the present day; registers of births, marriages and deaths; letters.

2 The teacher explained that the purpose of the activity was to produce a booklet containing a plausible story which made use of real people and situations.Although it would be heavily dependent on the source material, inferences and deductions were to be made.

To focus the work and avoid confusion, each group had to carry out careful preparations. Using the information they had acquired from their work on Victorian England, they had to draft a possible storyline. Then, using the knowledge they had gained about sources, they worked out which ones might be useful for developing their storyline.

3 Sources were allocated to different pupils in the group. Individuals in a group then worked on their sources to extract information. They were encouraged to integrate information from different sources to produce character sketches or mini-biographies about people, as well as to acquire details about houses, streets, occupations, etc.

4 The teacher used the research time to ask individuals questions which focused particularly on the reliability of the sources they were using and the inferences they could make about both the sources and the information contained therein.

Sufficient time was allowed for the research. Note-making skills were also fostered.

5 Once pupils had acquired sufficient information, the groups started to piece it together into a story, finally producing it in booklet form (see example in Figures 2.8.and 2.9)

6 The finished booklets were then passed around the class and read by other groups. Pupils were asked to evaluate critically the realism of the story and to say whether they felt any aspects were anachronistic or inaccurate. Each group wrote a brief critique on one other group's work.

This activity shows progression over the Key Stage 1 example (Example 2.5) in a variety of ways. In Key Stage 2:

■ pupils can work more independently and collaboratively both in posing questions and in planning and organising the communication. Less guidance was given throughout;

■ the range of source material is more extensive and demanding. There is more written material and pupils must devote time to selecting relevant material from long extracts. They have to choose what information is relevant;

■ pupils are expected to make links and connections between pieces of information in different sources. These include documentary sources as well as resources in libraries, textbooks and videos;

■ they have to consider the reliability of the evidence and what can be safely deduced and what cannot;

■ the final product is more extensive requiring the organisation of disparate material and communication skills, e.g. use of paragraphs, headings, extended writing;

Figure 2.8

That night Sarah came in looking very sad.

Thomas Penrose asked Sarah what was wrong and she replied "a boy tripped the inspector up ."

"He did WHAT?"shouted Thomas. "Tripped the inspector up? I thought you could look after them!"

Sarah was given her notice on the spot.

Figure 2.9

■ the historical knowledge and understanding expected is greater than in Key Stage 1. The historical content is less personal and pupils are expected to have a reasonable contextual knowledge of Victorian England.

All the examples above are designed to foster pupils' historical skills as well as developing their understanding of the historical content. It will also be obvious that throughout this process pupils are developing a wide range of general learning skills which are relevant throughout the curriculum.

General learning skills

It can be argued that there are very few skills which are unique to the study of history. Even such activities as evaluating sources or describing and explaining how things have changed over time are not uniquely historical tasks. Part of history's relevance to the primary curriculum is the way it develops a range of general learning skills. For example:

■ posing questions;

■ forming hypotheses;

■ extracting information;

■ recording information;

■ recalling information;

■ analysing information;

■ critically assessing information;

■ synthesising information from different sources;

- discarding irrelevant information;
- dealing with conflicting information;

- using imagination;
- making inferences and deductions;
- looking at different viewpoints;
- comparing and contrasting;
- making links and connections;
- predicting outcomes;
- explaining outcomes;

- listening skills;
- observational skills;
- group skills;
- speaking skills;
- writing skills.

You can probably add to this list.

Summary

We hope that it will be obvious from these examples that whilst historical content is always important, it is equally vital that all teachers give thought to what pupils do with that content. There is some value in pupils having a grasp of key events and people in the past, but the teaching must go beyond passing on that information in a passive way. In the best history teaching the content is *used*; the pupils are active participants rather than passive recipients. If the teacher has put in more effort in the classroom than the pupils, it is likely that the pupil experience has been too passive. Good primary history involves pupils doing much of the work!

'What is the best way to plan?'

2.2 Approaches to planning

Although the review of the history curriculum does not *require* that you start from scratch with your plans for history in Key Stages 1 and 2, it may involve some rewriting and provides an ideal occasion to take stock of the effectiveness of existing plans.

Many planning schemes were introduced hurriedly in schools in the early days of the National Curriculum. Some were imposed on schools by their choice of resources. Others were centrally planned and did not leave individual teachers sufficient flexibility to adapt the study units to their own style of teaching. Many plans laid too much emphasis on content and not enough on process.

The Annual Report of HMCI dealing with standards and quality for 1993/94 (based on OFSTED reports through the year) was critical of current planning in around half the schools in Key Stage 1 and rather more in Key Stage 2. It found that curriculum policies were in place but that they were not being translated into effective schemes of work and, in particular, that the schemes of work were not sufficiently detailed to ensure progression and continuity from year group to year group.

Against this background we see it as an important objective over the next few years to improve the planning of primary history. In this chapter we investigate possible approaches to long-term, medium-term and short-term planning.

Long-term planning

Long-term planning creates a **framework** for the whole curriculum. This will almost certainly be compiled and discussed by the whole staff. It will summarise the whole curriculum across each key stage showing sequences, balance, links and continuity.

As regards history in Key Stage 2, it will typically allocate each study unit to a given year group, ideally ensuring that each year pupils receive a meaningful experience of history; while in Key Stage 1 it will identify opportunities for history within the overall topic structure.

The main decisions facing teachers at the framework stage are:

1 **How discrete history should be.** All the evidence suggests that history in primary schools has become more distinct as a result of the introduction of the National Curriculum. However, very few schools have timetabled discrete history.

   This would make little sense in Key Stage 1 where the programme of study lends itself so well to a closely integrated and thematic approach in which pupils are introduced to their own personal history and that of the locality, they hear or read stories from history and they develop basic skills of sequencing and using sources.

   In Key Stage 2 the division into study units has resulted in a less integrated approach. Even so, the most common approach is to adopt topics which are heavily subject-based. A few schools adopt a completely discrete approach to history, but the majority use the umbrella of a given history study unit to encompass work in many other curriculum areas. Some also try to include opportunities for history in every topic, even when it is not history led.

2 **Whether to space history regularly through a given year or to have a 'history burst'.** The 'history burst' approach clearly allows for study in depth. It also allows for the closer linking of two related units. The Dearing review assumed a notional time for history of 45 hours per year in Key Stage 2. If this time is too spread out over a year, some of the momentum and clarity will be lost.

   On the other hand, the overall coherence of the history curriculum will be threatened if there are long gaps without any history. There will be so many strands to be picked up each time a history unit is tackled that valuable time will be lost. As our own rule of thumb, we feel it is probably bad practice for children to go two or more terms without some experience of history.

   Most schools will already have an effective framework in place. In deciding how appropriate it now is to the new orders the important consideration is that the framework is essential as it will determine how effectively coherence and progression can be achieved in the individual subject when teachers move on to medium-term planning.

AN APPROACH TO PLANNING

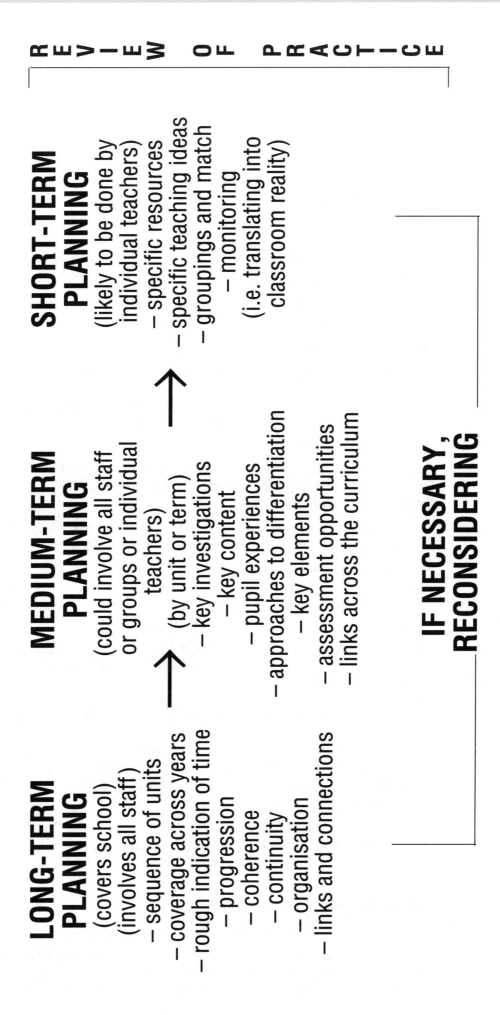

REVIEW OF PRACTICE

LONG-TERM PLANNING
(covers school)
(involves all staff)
– sequence of units
– coverage across years
– rough indication of time
  – progression
  – coherence
  – continuity
  – organisation
– links and connections

MEDIUM-TERM PLANNING
(could involve all staff
or groups or individual
teachers)
(by unit or term)
– key investigations
  – key content
  – pupil experiences
– approaches to differentiation
  – key elements
– assessment opportunities
– links across the curriculum

SHORT-TERM PLANNING
(likely to be done by
individual teachers)
– specific resources
– specific teaching ideas
– groupings and match
  – monitoring
(i.e. translating into
classroom reality)

**IF NECESSARY,
RECONSIDERING**

Medium-term planning

Medium-term planning typically focuses on structuring half-term or one-term **topics** or units from within the framework. It is where teachers currently direct most planning energy.

Medium-term planning may well involve the whole school but it is more likely to be the province of individual teachers or year groups, with input from the relevant coordinator.

Medium-term planning should summarise the main content, skills and conceptual areas to be covered within a topic; which teaching and learning approaches are to be used; and what assessment opportunities are to be created. The planning matrix on page 33 is a tool to help you do this.

The degree of flexibility teachers aim for in their plans will vary. Some teachers, especially non-specialists, welcome very tight planning. Others like plenty of flexibility to allow for the unexpected. Good planning should certainly aid exciting teaching and learning and not inhibit it.

For a topic with a strong history base, two aspects of planning are important:

■ deciding how to tackle the history aspect;

■ integrating work on other curriculum areas into the topic.

KEY STAGE 1

The Key Stage 1 curriculum has always been flexible and time problems have not been common. However, planning is no less important in making the most of the time available.

A one-page planning sheet (see page 31), in which the distinctive contributions of each of the curriculum subjects to the overall topic are made explicit, is the best starting point.

Ensure that the entry for history includes coverage of the key elements as well as any particular story, event or person you might be focusing on.

Ensure also that the Key Stage 1 topics taken together give a broad and worthwhile coverage of all the key elements – the requirement of the National Curriculum is that the key elements are during through the key stage.

A detailed account of how a Key Stage 1 topic on Myself and my family might be planned to maximise the usefulness of the history component is given on page 80.

KEY STAGE 2

Many teachers felt there was too much content to cover in Key Stage 2 under the old National Curriculum. Whether this problem has been adequately dealt with in the revised National Curriculum is partly a matter of opinion. But it is also a matter of planning – because the new flexibility in the KS2 curriculum can be used effectively only if coherent planning is undertaken.

Within the notional time of 45 hours a year for history in Key Stage 2 there is a real risk that without good planning important aspects of each history unit will be omitted or, worse still, covered but so superficially as to be of little use.

The following is our recommended planning strategy in Key Stage 2.

STAGE 1

The starting point is the overall framework (see page 28).

STAGE 2

Work out how much time is likely to be available for teaching this unit. Be realistic. Dearing hints at 20–25 hours per unit, but each unit may not require exactly the same amount of time devoted to it. The core/extension

TOPIC TITLE: OUR SCHOOL

ENGLISH	MATHEMATICS	SCIENCE
Discussion – our school, who fits where?	Shape – buildings windows door frames	Buildings – construction materials Weathering
Descriptions of buildings, play areas		
Who comes into/works in our school?	Time – set times sequencing times	
What do we do in school?		
Drama – the school day 'now' and 'then'		

IT	D & T	HISTORY	GEOGRAPHY
DTP	Model of school Design of room	'Then and now' – guest speakers Photographs Compare new and old building Playground games	Plans of building Mapping People who work there and their jobs

RE/MORAL EDUCATION	ART/CRAFT	MUSIC	PE
Clothes – protective old hygiene – toilet block	Observational drawing Textures – rubbings Shape pictures	Playground songs Music hall	Playground games PE – old and new

distinction has disappeared in the revised National Curriculum, but for planning purposes some units will still need more time than others.

You could establish a school policy on this, for example that the shortest unit takes no less than half the time you take over the longest unit. You must try to do justice to each unit.

STAGE 3 Decide how far a given unit can be combined with another unit. This is more feasible following the review. List areas of overlap.

This stage should not be seen simply as a time-saving exercise. It is also an important part of planning for coherence and progression, and for making links between units (one of the specific requirements of the key elements). For example, the local history option can obviously fit well alongside the British history units; Ancient Egypt (from the non-European list) can complement the Ancient Greece unit very effectively; the Aztecs (again from the non-European list) can complement and contrast with the Tudor Times British unit.

STAGE 4 Consider whether there are overlaps between a history unit and other curriculum areas which could free some time.

This is not essential, but well-planned development of other curriculum areas alongside history can be worthwhile. In Section 4 of this book we investigate these links in detail for each unit and on pages 37–42 we look particularly at history's potential for helping with the teaching of art, music and information technology.

Ensure that the links serve the needs of both history and the other subject. Guard against compromising any subject in order to squeeze everything in.

STAGE 5 Look at the focus statement for the unit. This will form the best summary of the content of the unit.

STAGE 6 Examine the content listed in the study unit. Choose a couple of aspects which you feel would make good areas for more detailed treatment. Remember that you will not be able to treat everything in the same detail. You should isolate approximately three areas for treatment in depth; the other areas should be treated in outline.

The following should help you decide on the areas for detailed examination:

■ the focus statement for the unit;

■ areas where the school is suitably resourced;

■ areas in which pupils are likely to be interested;

■ areas which might be suitable for investigative work by the pupils;

■ areas suitable for developing certain key elements on which you wish to focus.

Identify key questions that you would like to use to address the content areas you have selected (see Section 4 of this book).

At this stage the planning matrix on page 33 can be used.

The aims of this approach are:

■ to provide sufficient detail about the unit whilst still allowing some flexibility within the basic framework;

■ to encourage an active approach to history, putting emphasis on pupil experience;

■ to highlight the key ideas and messages that pupils should acquire;

■ to highlight links between units.

COLUMN 1: MAIN INVESTIGATIONS Each unit is broken down into questions or investigations which together cover the content and process (or key element) requirements.

The key questions flow from the focus statements.

The questions could equally be sub-headings, but questions encourage a more active investigative approach. A key question-based approach is much more likely to achieve good coverage of the key elements because the key questions can be oriented towards the concerns of the key elements; for example, 'why?' questions focus on reasons and results, but 'how do we know?' questions focus on sources of information.

Experience suggests that there should not be too many 'main investigations' although much will depend on the length of time being devoted to a unit. Four to seven key questions is often appropriate.

You should not spend equal amounts of time on each key question for the reasons outlined on pages 30–31 (Stage 2).

MAIN INVESTIGATIONS	KEY CONTENT	PUPIL EXPERIENCES	DIFFERENTIATION	KEY ELEMENTS	ASSESS. OPPS.	LINKS

COLUMN 2: KEY CONTENT FOR EACH MAIN INVESTIGATION

The second column should provide more detail on what content might be associated with each investigation. This can be done in the form of sub-questions or descriptions of content (see Section 4).

The degree of detail can be adapted to suit the needs of teachers. At the very least, it needs to embrace the required content, drawing attention to particular names, places, dates, events and situations.

COLUMN 3: PUPIL EXPERIENCES

This heading is carefully chosen to emphasise that this column is about what the pupil does rather than what the teacher does. It should contain three components (they could have been three separate columns but because they are so closely interlinked we prefer to include all three aspects in a single column).

1 **What the children will actually be doing.** This could give precise details of the activity to be undertaken, or simply an indication of the approach to be used, e.g. research task, fieldwork, source evaluation exercise, etc.

   The important thing is to ensure that the pupil experiences help foster the skills and understanding demanded in the key elements and level descriptions.

2 **What resources they will be using.** Also included in this column is reference to available resources. It makes little sense to devise learning approaches unless thought has gone into the types of resource which can be used. Again, include as much detail as necessary.

   The approaches to the study units in Section 4 (which use this same matrix format) include reference to a vast range of resources. You should aim to use an equally broad range of resources. If your list includes little more than a television series or a published book, valuable opportunities have been missed and the quality of the history experience for pupils is likely to be diminished.

3 **Any ways in which this pupil experience can be built on or linked with other history units.** You can be as general or as specific as you like, e.g. when looking at Tudor housing you could say 'Pupils compare with Roman housing', or simply 'Compare with another period'. The important thing is that making links and connections to other periods is seen as a key 'pupil experience'.

COLUMN 4: DIFFERENTIATION

If pupils have a part to play in choosing their own tasks, they will often differentiate for themselves, so in all the alternatives which follow you should bear in mind the need to allow pupils some choice in the tasks they attempt. Detailed descriptions of techniques for differentiation can occupy an enormous amount of time and space. As a result, we have developed for use in Column 4 the following coding system

1 Undifferentiated work – all pupils do exactly the same work and are expected to produce similar output. This is likely to be rare but could apply to a simple idea.

2 Differentiation by group – particular tasks are given only to some groups of pupils. Careful thought should be given to pupil groupings, and whether they are organised by friendship, gender or by ability.

3 Differentiation by outcome – the activities are given to all pupils, who produce answers at their own level.

4 Differentiation by task – some pupils are given simple and some more complex versions of the same tasks.

2.2 APPROACHES TO PLANNING

5 Differentiated source material – shortened or simplified sources are given to some pupils and a greater number or broader range of sources are given to others.

6 Differentiated resources – when researching tasks, certain pupils can be directed to certain books which best meet their needs.

7 Differentiation by teacher input – this is clearly the most common and effective form of differentiation. It could be applied to all activities, as teachers constantly provide the support needed for pupils to understand issues and be challenged in their thinking. However, we recommend using this only when this technique of differentiation is a deliberate strategy, e.g. on a particular activity where pupils are working fairly independently they may be told that the teacher is available for help if they want it.

8 Differentiation by time – this may mean that certain pupils are given longer to a complete a task or deal with some issue, while other pupils who complete work more quickly can be given further extension activities.

COLUMN 5: KEY ELEMENTS In this column you can either list the aspects of the key element which will be developed or apply the numbering system used in the Orders for History. Some activities will focus on a single strand of one key element, but others will embrace a range of strands and elements. The overall aim should be to give a reasonable and balanced coverage to the key elements over the key stage in question.

COLUMN 6: ASSESSMENT OPPORTUNITIES Recent SCAA guidance has stressed the importance of planning for assessment. This can also be organised using the matrix. In Section 4 a coding system is included for six different approaches to assessment. It is as follows:

A Examining the **everyday written work** done by pupils.

B **Special tasks** designed to focus on **specific objectives** but done informally as a normal part of teaching and learning.

C A **test or task** done more **formally**. This is relatively rare in the suggested planning sheets in Part 2 and is largely confined to the end of a study unit.

D **Observation** of everyday work in the classroom, particularly oral and group work.

E **Interviews/discussions** between the teacher and a single pupil or a small group of pupils. This will largely be done in the normal course of teaching. It could simply involve the teacher asking a pupil a question while he or she is engaged on a task, in order to assess the extent of his or her understanding and knowledge.

F **Self-assessment** and evaluation by the pupil. In some respects this is of a different order from other approaches to assessment, but it has validity and should be encouraged. It helps pupils to understand the criteria for assessment. The appropriate place for this type of assessment is often at the end of each study unit.

COLUMN 7: LINKS AND CONNECTIONS In many respects, the more detailed and precise the information in this column is, the more use it will be to teachers. A really detailed column would make precise references to each curriculum area, matching them to attainment targets and programmes of study. Whilst this can be extremely helpful, it can also be time-consuming and will require much space.

Instead, therefore, compromises may be needed. At its simplest, a reference would be made to other National Curriculum subjects. The examples in Section 4 go slightly further than this, suggesting possibilities beyond the mandatory subjects of the curriculum. Links are made to cross-curricular themes and dimensions such as Economic and Industrial Understanding, Environmental Awareness, Careers, Health Education, Citizenship (this is likely to be frequently relevant; some may prefer to refer to PSE) and Equal Opportunities. Because the links with English will be frequent and sometimes constant, it may be helpful to subdivide, e.g. into writing, reading, speaking and listening, drama, etc.

In the following chapter we highlight particular opportunities to build links between history and art, music and information technology.

STAGE 7 Make some general estimates of the time you wish to give to each area. Although strict time limits are probably undesirable, the time will run away with you if you do not make some estimates. For example, two depth studies each lasting seven hours would leave some eight to ten hours for outline treatment.

STAGE 8 Show your ideas to the history coordinator and other colleagues. Be prepared to refine and adapt in response to their comments and suggestions.

Short-term planning

The aim of short-term planning is to structure everyday teaching and assessment and to provide a detailed scheme of work for each week of the topic.

In many schools, short-term planning is often the weak link in the planning chain, sometimes not being done at all, or else consisting simply of rough headings. In its recent advice on planning (Planning the Curriculum at Key Stages 1 and 2 [1995]), SCAA advocates more detail in the short-term plan, e.g. describing differentiated activities.

Some schools produce fairly detailed fortnightly plans involving collaboration between teachers, which may be recorded quite formally, and then alongside these they may prepare daily plans which can be just rough notes in the teacher's file.

Medium-term planning provides detail about specific units but leaves teachers with a fair degree of flexibility. The purpose of short-term planning should be to give teachers an opportunity to state how they will translate that flexibility into their own specific teaching programme.

It could, for example, clarify:

■ exactly what resources they will be using;

■ what alternatives given in the matrix plans will be used (or better ones if they come to mind);

■ the main features of individual lessons;

■ how the particular work will be matched to different pupils in the class;

■ how the work will be monitored.

Schools vary in how they handle such short-term planning. It is likely to involve only individual teachers. The frequency may also vary from school to school, but it should happen at least weekly. Many teachers make daily jottings. As long as it is relevant and deals with useful issues, it does not have to be written down formally. Coordinators or headteachers may wish to see these plans, but their main function is to turn the medium-term plans into teaching practicalities dealing with the pertinent matters in each class.

'How helpful are history's links with other curriculum areas?'

2.3 Cross-curricular links

Schools are already well aware of history's links with curriculum subjects such as geography, science and English. Such links are further brought out in the matrices on pages 97–165.

However, we do want to offer some suggestions on less well-trodden paths – specifically, history's links with the art, music and IT curricula. These three subjects offer opportunities for developing the investigative skills required for history, particularly the handling of historical source material.

History and art

National Curriculum History can use a wide range of art from past and present and from different cultures, traditions and countries.

Photographs, paintings (of people, events, places), drawings, advertisements, ceramics, jewellery, textiles (including costumes), architecture and sculpture can all play an important part in history in both Key Stages 1 and 2.

Works of art can provide a starting point for discussion about an aspect of history, or can be an integral part of a full-scale historical investigation.

LOOKING AT CONTENT

A painting such as *Baby's Birthday* in Figure 2.10 can form an integral part of pupils' study of Victorian family life. Pupils can easily compare this household scene – furniture, family size, heating, lighting, costume – with the present day, or with contrasting pictures of family life in a different social class at a similar period. A painting such as this can provide pupils with many clues about the past and help them to reconstruct a given aspect of former times.

Figure 2.10

Similarly, a Greek vase often depicts a range of everyday activities which can give the pupils some insight into life in Ancient Greece.

LOOKING AT GENRE OR STYLE

Looking at the style of art at different times can give valuable insight into the materials and equipment used and the general level of technology of the time. Why, for example, were there suddenly so many black and white photographs for the Victorian period when these are absent from sources for the earlier periods the children will have studied? The answer, of course, lies in the invention of photography. The same question could be asked about the appearance of woodcuts in the Tudor period – the answer here lying in the invention of printing.

LOOKING AT ARTISTS' INTENTIONS

Questions about the intentions of the artist in creating a work (for example, whether it is a work of imagination or documentary) can be common to both history and art curricula. Pupils can readily discuss whether *Baby's Birthday* is a real scene or an imagined one. Such questions about the artist and his/her reasons for producing a work of art not only lead to a greater understanding of the life, work and times of a particular artist, but also expose pupils to higher levels of understanding of historical interpretations and representations.

Deeper questioning and investigation of the artist's intentions when creating a particular work could lead to some quite advanced historical tasks on interpreting evidence. For example, pupils can study the many portraits of Elizabeth I between the age of thirteen and her death. The early portraits, painted before she became queen, have a different intention from those painted when she was queen; in the later paintings the propaganda purpose took over. The Rainbow Portrait, for example, shows her at age 67 (three years before her death) looking significantly younger and more beautiful than she does in the portrait of her in her early twenties. Pupils could investigate why these portraits were painted (to bolster her reputation when large parts of the country were perpetually threatening to rebel). During her reign, Elizabeth never travelled to the north of England, partly because of fear of rebellion, but her portraits went to all corners of the country.

Tudor portraits are also full of symbolism. An appreciation of the use of symbolism in pictures, and a realisation that evidence from the past should not always be taken at face value, is a valuable development of pupils' historical skills as well as an important theme in evaluating works of art within the art curriculum.

This type of investigation can lead to art activities on portraiture, expression and composition.

To sum up, many of the visual sources used for history offer a valuable starting point for work within the art curriculum. As art is a 'content-free' subject, many teachers are finding value in linking works of art into both their history and art work.

History and music

Music played as important a part in the lives of ordinary men and women in many periods of the past as it does today. Pupils will therefore be able to find out many things about people of the past through their songs and music.

Pupils should experience the music themselves – not simply find out about it – which makes it most likely that music will play a part in examining later periods of history, as it is music from these periods that is available commercially.

STORIES OF COMPOSERS AND MUSICIANS

Stories of the lives of composers and other musicians could form a valuable part of history work.

At Key Stage 1 teachers might select a famous musician or composer for an in-depth study in order to fulfil the requirements to investigate the life of a famous person. At the same time pupils will gain an insight into the place of music in society at that time.

SONGS

There are many songs which tell stories. From the Victorian period, broadsides, folk songs and music hall songs tell different stories of urban and rural life. There are songs about the sea, factories, agricultural depression, coal mining, the iron industry, building canals and railways, experiences of poverty and stories of crime and punishment (such as poaching and transportation).

In Victorian schools songs were used to teach children 'correct' attitudes about empire and social life and to teach Christianity. Indeed, many religious songs sung by Victorian children are still in modern hymn books!

Nursery rhymes often have a narrative basis in historical events. Iona and Peter Opie have compiled a very thorough dictionary of nursery rhymes which traces these historical roots (see Select Bibliography).

If you can find local songs, or songs which detail local events, these can be used in a local history unit.

MUSICAL STYLES

Particular styles of music were usually developed for a particular purpose. Music that is characteristic of a period can therefore give insight into that period: early church music, Tudor madrigals and music hall songs are all evocative of a period and can help pupils build up more empathy for those periods.

The changing styles of music since the 1930s can interest pupils, as well as providing easily accessible recordings which can be analysed for mood, attitudes to the music, and the way they represented their age. Schools studying Britain Since 1930 often end the unit with a presentation which is accompanied by appropriate music.

INSTRUMENTS

Each society had its own favourite instruments, determined both by the technology of the time and by taste and wealth. The Horniman Museum in South London, for example, has an impressive array of instruments from the past and present, and from various cultures, and runs hands-on sessions for schools.

Even if pupils cannot themselves handle instruments from the past, they can hear their sounds on commercial recordings and can find many depictions of those instruments in sources from the past – Greek vases, for example, often portray a range of percussion and stringed instruments.

This can lead to pupils developing their own compositions on various instruments from different periods.

To sum up, music can be used to evoke many historical periods, giving pupils an added dimension to their study. History is all too often about reading and seeing. Pupils may not be able to hear the sound of everyday life in a Victorian street, but they can hear the sounds of Victorian songs.

History and information technology

DATA HANDLING

Information technology takes many forms and can successfully support the teaching of history in a variety of ways in both key stages.

Computer-based programs can allow for storage and retrieval of historical information. JUNIOR PINPOINT and OUR FACTS enable pupils to handle complex data in a manageable form. Census records are widely used by primary children when studying local history and Victorian times. Other records which are appropriate for information technology activities are trade directories, registers, memorials and gravestones, population and other lists, school registers, family history information, archaeological site information and place names.

To make these records more readily accessible, information contained in them can be entered into a database (by teacher or children). It can then be searched in order to extract relevant information about changing trends over a period of time and/or features of a particular issue or period, for example types of job prevalent in a particular place at a particular time.

The more powerful computer software packages such as JUNIOR PINPOINT not only include the storage and search facility but also allow pupils to communicate historical information in the form of computer-generated graphs and tables.

DATA COLLECTION – LOCAL HISTORY

OUR FACTS can be used by pupils in Key Stage 1 to collect data about themselves and to record this information.

JUNIOR PINPOINT includes a questionnaire facility whereby pupils can compile a questionnaire or data collection sheet linked to their area of study. This might be used on a site visit to investigate the functions of a room, defence systems, building materials, etc.

Back at school the information can easily be transferred from the data collection sheet to the computer and used in the form of a data file from which children can identify, sort and analyse information. Due to time pressures, it would have been impossible to carry out these tasks on site.

The process of collecting and analysing data, and then presenting findings using data-handling programs, helps develop skills in historical enquiry and communication.

HISTORICAL COMMUNICATION

There is a wide range of programs available which enable pupils to develop their skills in word processing, desktop publishing and generating computer graphics. Programs such as PENDOWN enable pupils to present work and edit it. The wide range of fonts and layout facilities makes it possible for pupils to present their findings in the style of a historical document or in the style of the time. For example, pupils might use a painting of a family at home to extract information about the household appliances and furnishing, and then present the findings in the form of a 19th-century inventory.

SOURCE ANALYSIS

One use of the word processing facility is in developing an understanding of interpretations. If written sources can be accessed on screen, pupils can be asked to highlight or delete biased sections in historical accounts. This can be done much more easily on screen than by using hard copies or by constant rewriting and copying.

CONCEPT KEYBOARD

For pupils with learning difficulties the use of the concept keyboard is invaluable. Programs such as STYLUS, WHAT'S THAT PICTURE? and PROMPT/WRITER allow teachers to produce a set of key words or phrases related to the history work being covered for use on the computer in writing activities.

Concept keyboard overlays are also useful in Key Stage 1. Those such as CONCEPT WRITER can help develop a sense of sequence, with sentences on screen being cut and pasted onto overlay pictures. Programs such as TOUCH EXPLORER PLUS allow photographs and drawings, such as pictures of buildings and aerial photographs of archaeological sites, to be examined and questioned.

GRAPHICS

Graphics programs such as ARTISAN and PRO-ARTISAN are very powerful and enable pupils to record their findings pictorially. Programs can be used successfully to support pupils during activities aimed at developing observational skills. Pupils could make observational drawings of artefacts or could 'translate' information from written sources into pictorial form: for example, translating a description of a castle in its heyday into a grand plan. This grand plan could then be compared with commercially published diagrams of the same place, and the question of authenticity versus artistic licence could be debated.

Graphics programs enable pupils to record features of particular times in the past which could then be displayed on a timeline to show change over time, for instance ship design over 1000 years. Alternatively, each group of pupils in the class could select just one aspect of the period they are studying, research it and present it pictorially. All pictures could then be displayed to reinforce the contemporaneity of artefacts, buildings, etc. of a particular time in the past.

Desktop publishing allows text and graphics to be used together on a computer.

SIMULATIONS

Sherston Software produces some successful archaeological simulations on the Vikings, the Romans and the Egyptians. They give a valuable insight into the process of archaeology.

Pupils are provided with the opportunity to select an archaeological site to excavate. After choosing the appropriate tool(s) with which to dig, objects (often in fragmented form) are discovered. Pupils can then ask the computer to reconstruct the object and give information about its origins and use. There is also a facility for storing information about the excavation in a journal.

Another popular archaeological program is UNEARTHING THE PAST, based on the Coppergate excavations in York.

Other computer-based historical simulations are of varying quality and they need to be reviewed with care. A number exist for most study units in Key Stage 2.

TIMELINES

Various timeline programs exist which develop pupils' sense of chronology. For example, TIME LINES by SOFT TEACH and TIME TRAVELLER: TUDORS AND STUARTS by ESM allow pupils to place information and analyse the Tudor period. This can help foster an understanding of change and development.

CD-ROM

CD-ROM is still very much at an experimental stage as far as contributing successfully to the development of historical knowledge and understanding is concerned.

CD-encyclopedias such as Hutchinson's *Encyclopedia* (Acorn) are gaining in popularity. Whilst few primary schools can afford some of the new CD-ROMs, they are appearing for topics such as the Saxons and Vikings.

OTHER TECHNOLOGY

The prevalence of computer technology should not obscure the value of more conventional technologies in historical education.

For example, pupils should be encouraged to record information at local sites on video. It reduces the time needed to record information on site and allows the evidence gathered to be used in later activities. Videos shot on site could be used as a stimulus for written work or drama. Pupils could put together a commentary for the video based on their historical investigations.

Still photographs – particularly slides – can be used in the same way. Pupils could be asked to photograph evidence that their local area has undergone change over the last 100 years.

The tape recorder will also be useful in oral history. Often, when children are involved in an 'interview' situation, for example with an elderly member of the community, they can forget important elements of the conversation. Recording information on tape allows for easy retrieval at a later date.

During fieldwork activities, children could tape their discoveries or impressions of a particular place.

Audiotape can also be used to help those who have problems with reading. This may not just be less able pupils. You could make a sound recording of a difficult document, enabling pupils to follow a semi-legible photocopy of a historical source.

To sum up, technology can help take some of the 'fatigue' out of manipulating historical data. It can also provide a range of tools for building pupils' conceptual understanding of the past and their skills of observation and analysis.

Issues in implementing National Curriculum History

'What should the history coordinator be doing?'

3.1 The role of the history coordinator

So far we have concentrated on planning issues. Turning those plans into reality will raise a number of questions which need particular discussion. The first concerns the role of the history coordinator.

Prior to the introduction of the National Curriculum, it was rare to find a coordinator for history in a primary school. Now most primary schools have one. In larger schools there are likely to be enough teachers for each teacher to focus on one curriculum area. In other schools, however, there has to be some doubling up. Trying to define the role of a coordinator, therefore, is very difficult. It will depend very much on the coordinator's other commitments, but the following variables will also be important:

■ the expertise in history of the rest of the teaching staff. If the majority of teachers in the school are either specialist and/or confident, the role will be less demanding.

■ the presence or absence of reward. It is rare to find permanent incentive points for coordinating history but, in the few cases where they do exist, it is realistic to demand more from the postholder than where they do not.

The advice that follows, therefore, needs to be seen in context. We are assuming the coordinator teaches in a large primary school and does not have multiple responsibilities. That does not make it invalid for those with multiple responsibilities: there simply needs to be an appropriate focusing on the key tasks.

It is highly desirable that the same person coordinates history across both Key Stages 1 and 2. Otherwise, there will be a wasteful duplication of effort and limited attention given to progression.

Understanding the requirements of the history order

Although there may be limited time, this should be a priority. If nothing else, it is quite likely that the coordinator will be expected to summarise for his or her colleagues the main features of the order (see pages 2–4)

Ideally the coordinator should also become familiar with any non-statutory guidance or subsequent legislation such as assessment and reporting arrangements. Part of the coordinator's role will clearly involve communicating such developments to others in the school, e.g. at staff meetings, on paper or through the use of staff-room noticeboards.

The coordinator should also have the expertise to advise on ways in which history can contribute to other curricular areas, including cross-curricular areas such as information technology (see pages 37–42).

Preparing the school's documentation for history

This will be a central feature of the work of the coordinator. The place of a curriculum policy for history and other documentation is covered on pages 50–54.

Managing the school's history resources effectively

Primary schools contain a mass of resources, many of them internally produced. Some have been around for many years and by no means all are appropriate for the new curriculum.

Coordinators should consider it part of their role to advise on the suitability of the existing tasks and resources, and to make their colleagues aware of what is available in the school. This could be done through setting up 'resource boxes' (see Example 3.1: Managing Resources below).

They should also assist colleagues in making the school-generated resources more suitable.

Published resources provide both teaching ideas and collections of relevant source material. It should be the coordinator's role to advise on purchasing decisions. Below you will find an example of a set of criteria used by one school for deciding what resources to buy.

To ensure the continued relevance of the resource boxes, coordinators should produce regular updated lists of what is available and what has been added to the box. Initially this is a time-consuming activity, but if it is put on a database subsequent work might involve only a simple updating.

See also the advice on the History Curriculum Handbook below (page 51).

EXAMPLE 3.1: MANAGING RESOURCES

Background
One school became concerned that its resources were so dispersed that teachers rarely knew what resources for a given subject existed in their own classroom, let alone elsewhere in the school.

Things came to a head during one professional development day when the teachers were asked to devote an hour to searching their teaching rooms for all the mathematics equipment they had. This was then brought to the hall and gathered together on the floor. The staff were amazed not just at the quantity but at the amount of duplication.

They therefore planned a more systematic approach to resources for each subject. Tight financial budgeting also encouraged them in their mission.

The role of managing resources was given to coordinators. It was recognised that changes would have to be made gradually.

Managing the history resources
For Key Stage 1, resource boxes were created for each of the topics the school was covering. In Key Stage 2 it was decided to have a large resource box for each study unit.

After some discussion, it was decided to locate the resource boxes in the staff-room which, fortunately, was large enough. Another local school was even more fortunate in having a separate resources area.

The main aim was for the resource boxes to be used frequently. This meant that:

■ only genuinely useful material should go into the box;

■ all teachers should be clear about what the resource boxes contained.

A common format for each unit was agreed by teaching staff.

Each resource box contained:

■ a summary of the main content;

■ teaching suggestions, especially with regard to the coverage of the key elements, e.g. specific historical terms, specific skills and concepts, interpretations;

■ suggested assessment activities and marking approaches;

■ teaching plans for different year groups incorporating the particular unit;

■ a copy of each of the main books used in the school for that unit;

■ a list of other books available elsewhere, e.g. in the library, with a brief description of the format and nature of the book and where it could be found;

■ copies of written source material, including photocopies of original sources and simplified transcripts where necessary;

■ for many sources, suggested questions which could be posed about the sources;

■ relevant visual sources such as slides, pictures, paintings;

■ a summary of posters and artefacts available in the school with suggestions as to how they can be used and where they could be found (there was insufficient room in the boxes to keep them there);

■ relevant music cassettes;

■ computer software;

■ a list of possible sources of information outside the school, including places to visit, people who might be interviewed, useful contacts;

■ copies of evaluations of past work by teachers or pupils.

If circumstances allow, the contents of the box can be summarised on a database and the contents included in the resource box. This can be updated occasionally as resources are added to the box.

Helping colleagues develop subject expertise

This is a major difficulty in many schools. However, it is consistently demonstrated that the best history is taught in classrooms where the teacher has a good grasp of the content and processes associated with the subject.

It can never be the role of the coordinator to develop detailed subject awareness. However, without some awareness, teachers will struggle to make the subject interesting. It takes some expertise to know what is significant and what is interesting. The knowledgeable teacher will be able to identify the key ideas in a unit and concentrate on those, and will therefore avoid overwhelming his or her pupils. The French philosopher, Pascal, once apologised for writing a long letter to a friend, explaining that he did not have time to write a short one.

The main aim of Section 4 (pages 79–165) is to help each teacher to identify the key ideas, people, situations, events and sources of information related to particular study units. This section should help to increase your colleagues' confidence in handling each history study unit.

Training may be available for staff. If so, part of the training arrangements should be to consider how the skills and information learned can be disseminated effectively to colleagues.

After attending a 20-day history course, one coordinator was keen that all teachers in the school should adopt a consistent and worthwhile approach to the different concepts. She therefore prepared for her colleagues a brief pack covering each of the following concepts:

■ causation: reasons and results;

■ change and chronology;

■ interpretations and representations.

Each pack contained the same basic elements:

■ a summary of the issues and key questions within each of the study units which were particularly appropriate for developing that concept area;

■ suggested activities presented as flexibly as possible which could be used to develop, reinforce and assess pupils' grasp of the concept;

■ some sample work from pupils together with the coordinator's comments on how far the pupil is demonstrating a grasp of the concept.

Monitoring and evaluating the effectiveness of the subject in the school

This is a difficult and sensitive area. There are good reasons to steer clear of it: it is the role of the headteacher or at least a senior member of staff to monitor such matters; teachers are often sensitive about colleagues poking their noses into their classrooms or teaching files; there is little time to carry out such monitoring.

Despite this, there are ways that coordinators can approach this task without either treading on colleagues' toes or increasing their workload substantially. Examples 3.2 and 3.3 explain two approaches.

EXAMPLE 3.2: MONITORING AND EVALUATION ARRANGEMENTS FOR HISTORY

1 All teaching plans for history are passed to the history coordinator.

2 The coordinator will pay particular attention to ensuring:

■ that the statutory curriculum has been covered;

■ that there is no unnecessary duplication;

■ that content and activities represent a manageable and interesting experience for pupils;

■ that the work across different years represents a reasonable progression in that subject.

3 Twice each year at staff meetings the coordinator will be responsible for organising and running a standardisation exercise. This will involve the selection of samples of pupils' work from different years. Copies will be made for teachers with the marks and comments removed. Teachers will then discuss the merits of the work and agree common grades using the school's assessment scheme.

The aim of this is to standardise assessment within the school.

4 Each year the coordinator will submit a brief report to the headteacher and governing body evaluating the successes and problems of history during the year.

5 Every effort will be made to free the history coordinator at least once per term to spend time working with another teacher. This remains flexible to coincide with occasions when history is being taught. Where such time is made available, the coordinator will discuss briefly in advance with the headteacher how they wish to use that time.It will be expected that this non-class contact time will be spent visiting different classes rather than revisiting the same class.

6 Coordinators will briefly examine the records noting pupil progress in the subject.

EXAMPLE 3.3: HISTORY COORDINATOR: MONITORING CHECKLIST

Please check and comment briefly on the following questions. Use this information to produce your annual report on developments and problems in the subject.

A. Staffing

1 What professional development have staff had in history during the past year?

2 Have there been meetings with history coordinators from other phases and schools?

3 If so, with whom? What was covered? How successful were they?

B. Curriculum

1 Have the planned number of study units been covered this year?

2 Has the coverage caused any difficulties in any classes?

3 If so, which and how?

4 In your view, has sufficient time been made available for history?

5 Has the planning been satisfactory?

6 Has the coverage of content, skills and processes improved in classes this year?

7 Has sufficient note been taken of the requirements addressed in the key elements?

8 Has the range of pupil experiences and assessment activities been satisfactory? Have the pupils been actively involved in history?

9 Have you been satisfied with the differentiation and progression within history?

10 Has the quality of display been good enough?

11 What use has been made of support services and facilities such as advisory teachers, museums, libraries, archives, buildings and sites, archaeologists, older citizens?

C. Management and organisation

1 How much have you been able to achieve in your role of coordinator?

2 What constraints have you faced?

3 How much funding has been available for history?

4 How does the sum per pupil compare to the last three years?

5 What type of thing has the money been spent on?

6 In your view, has the money been well spent?

7 Have you produced any new documentation for the subject during the year, e.g. curriculum guidance, resource lists?

8 How useful do you feel teachers have found them?

9 Has the profile of history been sufficiently high this year, e.g. within the school, amongst parents and governors?

10 Have you been satisfied with the quality of the recording of achievement in history and the reporting of progress to parents?

Liaising with teachers of the subject in other phases

There should be occasions when the coordinator will want to discuss common concerns, such as local visits etc., with those who teach in the schools to which pupils will transfer.

Primary–secondary liaison is not consistent nor always successful. However, if priority is attached to well-planned and regular if infrequent meetings, coordinators can save duplication of effort, share resources and share ideas.

Liaison need not be solely with other phases. It is equally important to meet fellow coordinators in the vicinity.

Producing reports on the subject when and if necessary

Some reports are likely to be regular: for example, coordinators may be asked for an annual report for the subject area (see Example 3.4 below for one included as part of a development plan).
Others may be more sporadic, such as brief reports on some history event for the school newsletter or on a curriculum development for governors.

It would be realistic to expect the coordinator to produce these reports.

Producing an annual development plan

This may be unrealistic in some schools, but in others it is an increasingly important area.

At the heart of the school development plan should lie the curriculum. Some schools are already asking for brief curriculum development plans from their coordinators which can contribute to the whole school development plan and help prioritise the many tasks that need to be done.

An example of an annual development plan is provided in Example 3.4 below. In the example the evaluation of the past year has been made the basis for setting future priorities.

Although the responsibility for this evaluation and the identification of needs is likely to rest largely with history coordinators, they might not be the only people involved in the process. Other teachers at staff meetings, governors and even parents should be encouraged to contribute ideas.

Subject coordinators should be brief when producing their development plan; the whole plan should fit onto one page. All the important issues should be included but they should be reduced to their essentials.

In setting future priorities it is important not to be too ambitious over timescales. There needs to be a reasonable balance of objectives across a period of time.

When defining priorities, short-term needs may not necessarily have the highest priority. Some urgent issues may need to be dealt with over a considerable period of time.

Costs also need careful consideration. As well as direct expenditure, it may be necessary, for example, to allow for cover teaching costs if one priority is training or professional development.

EXAMPLE 3.4: ANNUAL REPORT AND DEVELOPMENT PLAN

HISTORY AT XXX SCHOOL: 1993–94

Evaluation of 1992–93

History was taught in all year groups. We increased our range of resources by purchasing sets of the Ginn and Longmans materials. However, there were insufficient copies of books to allow use in whole–class situations. The amount of time devoted to history in Key Stage 1 was limited, especially in reception and Year 2, but the work done, especially on timelines and family history, went down well. In Key Stage 2 the Invaders and Settlers proved overwhelming in Year 3 and Ancient Greece caused some difficulties in Year 4. The most successful units were Victorian Britain and the local history unit, where some good work was done by Year 5 using trade directories and censuses. We also had a successful visit to the museum, and the local museum education officer came into school. We have built up local history source collections, especially some photographs and pamphlets, but these need to be extended. It was pleasing that the history coordinator was given half a day each half term to carry out duties in relation to this job.

Priorities for the coming year

1 Increase the range of resources, especially for the teaching of Ancient Greece (cost estimated . . .; responsibility of . . .; ideal completion by . . .).

2 Add 12 extra copies of pupils' readers for Core Units 1, 2 and 3a (cost estimated . . .; responsibility of . . .; ideal completion by . . .).

3 Attend an in-service training course run by the LEA on the teaching of Ancient Greece (cost estimated . . .; responsibility of . . .; ideal completion by . . .).

4 Lead a staff meeting discussing assessment strategies in Key Stages 1 and 2 history (responsibility of . . .; ideal completion by . . .).

5 Attempt to increase non-contact time by three days a year to spend time in other classrooms when history is being taught (responsibility of . . .; ideal completion by . . .).

6 Subscribe to the journal <u>Primary History</u> (cost estimated . . .; responsibility of . . .; ideal completion by . . .).

7 In conjunction with the headteacher, analyse the history plans for each topic and feed back to teachers suggestions for improvement, resourcing, etc. (responsibility of . . .; ideal completion by . . .).

8 Ensure that timelines appear in each classroom (responsibility of . . .; ideal completion by . . .).

Summary of resource implications
Cost of books, materials and equipment . . .
Staff time . . .

The three absolute priorities are:
1. . . .
2. . . .
3. . . .

Signed by . . .

Discussed with headteacher on . . .

Liaising with relevant organisations regarding history matters

It is a sensible policy to allocate the responsibility of liaising with those representing various history interests to the coordinator. These might be local support services such as museums, archives, sites and advisory teachers, inspectors or regional and national bodies such as SCAA.

Summary

These tasks may seem overwhelming. Indeed, if a coordinator tried to take them all on tomorrow they would be. Our purpose is not, however, to write a job description so much as to identify the dynamic role that could emerge for a history coordinator if time and resources allowed.

'What documentation should we have available for inspection?'

3.2 Documentation

There is currently an unhealthy concern with curriculum documentation. The prospect of OFSTED inspection probably lies behind much of this concern. There is a pervasive myth that schools will be praised in direct proportion to the weight of their curriculum documentation.

The truth is very different:

■ OFSTED and others have publicly said that they would prefer tatty bits of paper which refer to sensible policies, and which are well understood and applied, rather than extensive documentation, which is often incomprehensible and unfamiliar to most people in the school.

■ There is *no point at all* in having documents which do not ease the task of the teacher, reduce confusion and provide pointers to quality teaching and learning. If the documentation looks like bureaucracy gone mad, it probably will be and should be ditched.

■ Too much time has been wasted worrying about differences between policies, schemes of work, lesson plans, etc. What matters is the overall situation. If all that teachers need to implement the history curriculum fully can be combined in one document then that is to be welcomed. In Example 3.5 below the necessary guidance is gathered together as a sample handbook, *History Curriculum Guidance*.

EXAMPLE 3.5: HISTORY CURRICULUM GUIDANCE HANDBOOK

Ideally this 'handbook' should include all the necessary documentation – including a policy statement – and a copy should be given to all staff.

The example below is from a school which requires each coordinator to produce such a handbook for his or her given curriculum area.

Once it has been compiled on disc, keeping the handbook up to date became a relatively easy task. Only certain sections need updating. Old pages can be replaced with new ones without requiring a complete rewrite.

We do not have space to reproduce every section of the handbook. Instead we have included the sections not covered elsewhere in this book and simply summarised the sections which duplicate advice elsewhere (along with a page reference).

HISTORY CURRICULUM GUIDANCE

HANDBOOK 1994–95

Purpose of this Handbook
The aim of this handbook is to:
■ demonstrate the way history is taught in the school;
■ reduce ambiguity;
■ ensure a reasonable level of consistency amongst teachers in the school;
■ foster some stability and continuity irrespective of staffing;
■ increase efficiency;
■ improve teaching and learning;
■ provide a suitable framework for curriculum planning and assessment.

Contents

An introduction to history. What is distinctive about the subject?
The central concern of history teaching will always be people.
   Children studying history in Key Stages 1 and 2 should investigate the lives of men, women and children in different societies, religions, cultures and countries.
   They should examine how their lives changed and developed and how people interacted over time. They should investigate the reasons why people acted as they did and the changes which resulted from these actions.
   Pupils should understand that history is our record of what happened to people and why. Through historical enquiry, children should be given the opportunity to gather information and analyse and interpret this record.
   History is not value-free, but the teaching will aim to be as objective as possible. The following attitudes and values should be encouraged:

■ tolerance – the ability to look at people and situations with an awareness of their circumstances. It should not be equated automatically with sympathy;
■ a concern for truth and accuracy;
■ an appreciation of the diversity of humanity and the positive benefits of this diversity;
■ an appreciation and enjoyment of the past and present environment and the importance of the past to the present;
■ a sense of realism;
■ a sense of optimism through an understanding of one's roots and membership of the human race;

- initiative;
- perseverance;
- commitment.

A policy statement with regard to the teaching of history in the school

HISTORY CURRICULUM POLICY

It would be wrong to see the following as a definitive model. There are different but equally valid approaches. The following is only one possible approach.

A. THE NATURE OF HISTORY

Children studying history in Key Stages 1 and 2 should focus on men, women and children in different societies, religions, cultures and countries. They should examine how they developed and interacted over a period of time. Pupils should understand that history is our actual record of what happened and why. Through historical enquiry, children should be given the opportunity to gather information, analyse it and take into account the often uncertain nature of history before interpreting that record.

B. AIMS OF OUR HISTORY WORK

1 To cover the specific content determined by the National Curriculum programmes of study and as detailed in the school's scheme of work for history.

2 To develop the skills and conceptual understanding laid down in the orders, especially in the key elements section for Key Stages 1 and 2.

3 To make links with other curriculum areas where appropriate.

4 To contribute to basic skills and themes such as literacy, oracy, numeracy and information technology.

5 To arouse and sustain interest in history.

6 To emphasise the importance of equality of opportunity, particularly by contributing to the pupils' knowledge and understanding of people in other societies, religions, cultures and countries as well as their own.

7 To help pupils understand the present world in the light of the past.

8 To help pupils develop a sense of identity by learning about the development of the United Kingdom, Europe and the rest of the world.

C. THE TEACHING AND LEARNING OF HISTORY

1 The activities we plan should take account of the programmes of study including the knowledge, skills and concepts specified in the key elements, specified content and level descriptions for the relevant key stage.

2 History may frequently be delivered as part of a topic but the National Curriculum requirements will be made explicit in any planning. Planning for history will refer to the key areas for investigation, the principle content, pupil experiences including the appropriateness of activities for the ages and abilities of the pupils and the opportunities for assessment, resources and links and connections with other curriculum areas. The general coverage of history themes will be noted on the whole school framework and teachers will keep personal short-term plans.

3 At least one topic area each year will have a history focus. Some aspects of Key Stage 2 history will be taught as subject specific. The linking and sequencing of certain study units will be given particular attention in order to achieve coherence and continuity. The content of individual study units will not be broken up.

4 All key elements will be planned for and addressed at least once each year.

5 All pupils are entitled to an equal opportunity to achieve progress in history, irrespective of race, gender, social and economic circumstance or ability. Attention should be given to choice of texts and other resources. Whilst sensitivity is necessary to avoid giving offence to some groups or individuals, issues related to race and gender should be discussed in their historical contexts.

6 Planning should take account of the fact that progress in learning history is recursive not linear.

7 All work should stem from a discussion, visit, topical event or story which should be linked to a designated area of historical study.

8 There will be opportunities for a variety of pupil experiences including whole-class teaching, group work and individual work. There will be a strong emphasis on investigative work. Children should be encouraged to plan and carry out their own investigations using a range of appropriate resources including:
   a) written sources such as books, archive records, maps, newspapers, letters, diaries and inventories;
   b) visual and tangible sources such as photographs, artefacts, posters, paintings, buildings and sites, film, slides and video, and IT software;
   c) oral and aural sources such as tape-recorded interviews, stories, adults talking and music.

9 There will be opportunities for historical reconstructions in the form of music, dance, drama, debate and museum displays.

10 Children should be given the opportunity to select, organise and interpret historical information as individuals and as members of a group.

11 Pupils should be encouraged to question their findings and consider possible reasons for different versions of events.

12 Whilst some issues will be treated broadly to help pupils grasp overviews, each study unit will contain some issues (normally one to three) which will be looked at in depth.

13 Children should be encouraged to communicate and record their findings orally, visually and in various forms of writing.

14 Assessment of history will conform to the whole–school policy. It will normally form an integral part of the teaching and learning, and involve observing pupils at work, questioning, talking and listening to them and examining work produced by them. A range of assessment approaches for history should be planned, addressed and recorded . Records of achievement kept for history will conform to the policy on whole–school record-keeping.

15 Each classroom should contain:
   a) one historically-based display at least twice each year;
   b) a timeline around the wall;
   c) a collection of historical artefacts.

D. ADMINISTRATION

1 All teachers will contribute to the planning and delivery of history and to the assessment of progress in the subject.

2 The coordinator for history will:
   a) advise on plans, teaching and learning approaches, assessment and resources;
   b) submit an annual evaluation and development plan for the subject;
   c) monitor progression and differentiation within the subject;
   d) organise two staff meetings each year to discuss history issues including the standardisation of assessment;
   e) prepare and update documentation relevant to the teaching and learning of the subject;
   f) represent the school on matters relating to history;
   g) consult with those providing support for the subject beyond the school.

E. REVIEW

1 This policy will be reviewed at least every two years and updated as necessary.

2 This version dates from . . . when it was approved by the governing body following presentation by the history coordinator.

Comments
A policy statement should aim to be brief (one to three sides often suffices), realistic and achievable; it should be clearly written and provide positive direction as to what should be achieved without being over-prescriptive.

It should also be reviewed regularly and amended accordingly.

Clearly, any policy should relate to the general policies of the school and should conform both to the school's ethos and to the statutory requirements for history.

Good practice
(A summary statement outlining the main characteristics of good practice in history. See page 1.)

History curriculum organisation
(This includes a copy of the school's framework showing the order in which study units are taught – see Section 2.2.)

A history calendar
(This section of the guidance notes meetings where history will be discussed; known dates for courses; deadlines for reports; deadlines for the history development plan; dates of visits known in advance.)

Useful information
(This includes copies of any general letters and information which might possibly be useful on future occasions: for example, information about visit and special events such as displays, requests for artefacts for a class museum, copies of responses to national or local documents such as curriculum reviews.)

History coordinator: job description
(This school includes a copy of the job description for each coordinator in the relevant curriculum handbook. This helps other members of staff to know how the coordinator might be able to support them. See advice in Section 3.1.)

Professional development
(This includes details of recent staff development for history, including courses attended, training targets, visits by outside support such as advisory teachers, details of how information is disseminated and any evaluation of such professional development.)

Liaison
(This summary sheet outlines recent liaison arrangements with schools that provide or receive pupils, such as the infant and secondary schools. The information will refer to any records transferred for history, and the experience pupils have had in history from contributory schools, such as what units have been covered and when, what local history has been done and what visits they have had.)

Development plan
(The school includes a copy of the most recent history development plan, along with any targets set for history – see Example 3.4 on pages 49–50.)

Finance
(Alongside the development plan, this details how much has been spent on history during the last year with an indication of how the money has been spent and the sum available per pupil.)

3.3 Assessment

'Assessment is in total confusion. Exactly what are we supposed to do?'

Principles

There can be few primary schools which do not find assessment problematic. OFSTED, in its 1992–93 report, concluded that assessment was satisfactory in only a few primary schools. 'For the most part it was still at an early stage of development.'

At the current time, there is a particular dilemma in that schools have been left in limbo regarding assessment of the non-core subjects. In history the tick-box approach of the early years of the National Curriculum has been roundly condemned; and the curriculum review has done away with the detailed statements of attainment on which that system was based. Now schools have to devise their own assessment system, *but without real guidance on how to do it effectively*.

Schools still have to report to parents each year, giving brief details of progress in history and highlighting strengths and weaknesses, even if they are not reporting against any particular scale.

In our view an effective assessment scheme for primary history is both necessary and possible. In the system of assessment we are proposing below, we are aiming for assessment that is intelligible, coherent and manageable, based on the following principles:

1 Assessment opportunities must be planned.

2 Assessment will cover not just content requirements but also the key elements for Key Stages 1 and 2.

3 Pupil progress will be gauged by a variety of methods:

- marking everyday written work;

- setting specific assessment activities for history;

- observing pupils in action;

- talking with individual pupils.

4 Pupils will have opportunities for self-assessment and peer-group evaluation.

5 Wherever possible (hopefully almost always), assessment will be a normal part of teaching. Assessment will not be intrusive.

6 Information will be gathered only if it is really necessary. There is no point devoting time and effort to assessment if it does not improve teaching and pupil learning and, ultimately, lead to higher standards.

7 The results of the assessment must be comprehensible to and meet the needs of all those making use of it. This will avoid a situation where hours are devoted to recording achievement after which the records are placed in a filing cabinet and largely ignored by everyone.

8 Reliability is all important. Users must have confidence in the process. This means avoiding impression marking, having sound criteria and assessing in a range of contexts. One teacher's assessments should be checked by others.

9 Any records kept should be manageable and concise.

10 Reporting should be geared to the needs of the child and the parent.

A system of assessment

There is a dilemma in assessment. Any system of assessment has to be manageable: the more complex it is, the less likely it is to be used. However, any system also needs to be rigorous: the more simplified the scheme, the less reliable it is likely to be.

The scheme suggested below is intended to be realistic while being rigorous enough to be accepted as a fair and reliable system. It aims to be effective and efficient within the resources available to most primary schools.

STAGE 1: A WHOLE SCHOOL POLICY

This should already be in place and any procedures for history must fit within this.

STAGE 2: DEFINING ASSESSMENT OBJECTIVES FOR HISTORY

This will be the role of the coordinator for history. The objectives should relate predominantly to the areas of performance in the level description, which are themselves derived from the key elements.

Our suggested formulation of assessment objectives is shown in Figure 3.1. This can be photocopied onto the back of the class record sheet (see Stage 6).

Figure 3.1

ASSESSMENT OBJECTIVES FOR HISTORY

1 **Sense of time and chronology including, wherever appropriate, the ability to:**
   – understand and use relevant time terms;
   – sequence events, people and objects;
   – relate historical information to particular times;
   – distinguish between past times and between past and present;
   – use dates;
   – detect similarities and differences between periods;
   – identify changes that have occurred in history, and things that have continued unchanged between periods of history.

2 **Ability to recall or recount historical knowledge of:**
   – events;
   – ideas/beliefs/attitudes;
   – people;
   – situations;
   using historical vocabulary when appropriate.

3 **Ability to offer explanations for things that happened in history, giving reasons and results.**

4 **Understanding that history has been represented in different ways and the reasons for those different representations.**

5 **Ability to extract information from a range of historical source material:**
   – to use sources to pursue an investigation;
   – to comment on sources' reliability and usefulness for answering history questions.

6 **Ability to investigate historical questions including:**
   – organising material;
   – communicating accurately and in appropriate ways.

STAGE 3: PLANNING ASSESSMENT ACTIVITIES

This should take place as part of an individual teacher's medium-term planning.

The medium-term plan should record:

- what history will be assessed;

- where, within the teaching programme, the assessment will be done;

- what types of assessment will be carried out, e.g. everyday written work, special tasks, tests, observation, interviews, discussion, self-assessment.

The range of assessment opportunities identified should be broad enough to inspire confidence. If assessment is limited to dealing once with a given assessment objective, it will provide a most unreliable record of progress. Pupils' progress in history is sporadic. They may apply a skill in one context but not necessarily in another.

Even so, assessment should not overwhelm. Large chunks of history may have little or no assessment.

STAGE 4: CHECKING BY COORDINATORS

The coordinator, and possibly the headteacher, will check through the teacher's plans to ensure that assessment activities are manageable, realistic, appropriate to the ages and abilities and not repetitive, and show progression across different classes.

STAGE 5: DESIGN AND RUN ASSESSMENT ACTIVITIES

Teachers should be aware of the many factors that can affect the appropriateness of an assessment task. Some of these are summarised in the photocopiable list overleaf.

It would be helpful if the coordinator could build up a resource box of suitable activities which can be both a normal part of history teaching and also used to assess understanding of history objectives. This should be seen as a gradual task (see Stage 7 on page 62).

The coordinator should also be available to advise on any new activities designed for assessment. Do they:

- adopt a range of approaches;

- challenge the pupils;

- assess what they are supposed to assess;

- work in the time allocated;

- need further differentiation to suit the needs of the pupils?

As pupils undertake assessment activities teachers should be prepared to learn from experience and change tack if a particular line of assessment is not leading where it should.

STAGE 6: RECORDING

Teachers complete relevant records of history assessments. Our proposed recording scheme uses the sheets on pages 59-60. The principles are:

- to record enough to show what individual pupils are achieving, and to be able to compare that with class achievements;

- to record particular problems which pupils are facing in history;

- to record in such a way that everyone who needs the information can use it, i.e. it should provide easy ways into report writing, planning future work for an individual or a class, taking special action such as statementing, or providing details for a receiving school;

- to record at agreed intervals and by an agreed method.

Setting and running assessment tasks

Some questions to consider before setting or running assessment tasks:

1 **Time** – have you allowed enough time for all pupils to work at their own speed?

2 **Presentation** – great care is needed in setting out tasks clearly and making sure instructions and explanations are easily understood.

3 **Language** – the language used can influence performance significantly. History demands some high–level language skills. Pupils may work most easily in their own personal, spoken language, but their progress towards understanding and communication using more formal, abstract and compressed language should not be ignored.

4 **Challenge** – do not underestimate what pupils are able to achieve in history. High levels of thinking are often demonstrated at an early age. Do not be frightened of extending their thinking through investigative work, open-ended questioning, problem-solving, detective work, making inferences and deductions, making judgements and decisions, creative work, imaginative work, and discussion and debate.

5 **Revisiting skills and concepts** – pupils' progress may be sporadic, with no neat linear development. Historical understanding develops like a mosaic which needs gradual infilling. This means that it may be necessary to assess a skill using different content in order to be sure that the skill has been fully grasped and can be applied consistently.

6 **Range of contexts** – it helps if pupils can be involved in a range of tasks, including pair and peer group work. This is beneficial in encouraging pupils to think adventurously and to pose and test ideas.

7 **Equal opportunities** – when setting tasks, any issues relevant to equality of opportunity should be considered. Will some pupils respond better using some types of task or specific kinds of content, or when grouped in particular ways?

8 **Atmosphere** – it helps if a positive atmosphere can be engendered. Pupils can panic if there is an overplaying of the role and significance of assessment.

9 **Differentiation** – variation in pupils' historical competence can be considerable in many classrooms. Do not expect all pupils in a class to perform equally, nor individual pupils to perform consistently over different objectives or even across the same objective. Allow for differentiation in designing your tasks.

CLASS RECORD SHEET: Key Stages 1 and 2

Activities: (Use code numbers on planning sheets)

Class List	Objectives					
	1	2	3	4	5	6

....

....

....

....

....

....

....

....

....

....

....

....

....

....

....

....

....

....

....

Code

G – Good standards and rapid progress; above average for year and or capability (or green coded).
A – Standards and progress conforming closely to age/capability (or orange coded).
D – Difficulties noted, i.e. low standards, slow progress (or red coded).

Please add * if any explanation is provided on the individual pupil record sheet (or red coded).

INDIVIDUAL PUPIL RECORD SHEET:
Key Stages 1 and 2

Name . . . .

Study unit/year:

Study unit/year:

Study unit/year:

Study unit/year:

Study unit/year:

The class record sheet

In Key Stage 2 this is completed after each study unit. In Key Stage 1 it could serve as a yearly or termly sheet.The number of class record sheets would therefore average one to two per year.

It is important that whatever adaptations you make to the scheme, the assessment objectives remain consistent through out the school. In the example, we have used the objectives outlined in Stage 2 above. They have been presented in such a way that they can be photocopied onto the back of the class record sheet.

The information to be recorded on this sheet is:

1 **Activities** – this lists any particular assessment activities which you used to arrive at your judgements. As the tasks should already be described on your planning sheets simply use numbers to cross-refer to the planning sheet, e.g. 'Planned Assessment Activities 1–5'.

2 **Class list** – if the list of pupils' names is put on computer, it is clearly going to be quicker to prepare each new record sheet.

3 **Objectives** – if the unit has involved an explicit focus on certain objectives (as it almost always should), simply note your assessment against that objective (using the letter or colour code described at the foot of the sheet).

For pupils who have achieved a particularly high performance or have faced particular problems, a mark such as * refers users to further information on the Individual Pupil Record Sheet.

It is up to individual teachers to decide how to refer to and use specific pupil work in reviewing progress over the unit.

The individual pupil record sheet

Every pupil has an individual pupil record sheet which runs over a number of years, perhaps over the whole of a key stage or through a two-year cycle.

However, this is only completed *when necessary*. One of the questionable practices over recent years has been the meticulous recording of achievement for all pupils when the vast majority make steady progress and conform closely to what one would expect given their age and ability.

For many pupils there will be no comment made; some may go through most of their primary school career without significant comment. However, there will be occasions when some pupils perform in a way which is unexpected or unsatisfactory. It is in these circumstances that the individual pupil record sheet comes into operation. It provides teachers with an opportunity (but not an obligation) to explain or comment on rapid progress or lack of progress.

It is worth underlining our belief that, for assessment to be useful, it may be necessary to note what pupils cannot do as well as what they are able to achieve. Although this may seem unnecessary to some and for others may go against the grain, in that it adopts a less than wholly positive approach, it can be valuable in putting attainment in a wider context. It is surely of positive value to know what pupils cannot do very well and to let this influence subsequent teaching.

The type of information noted on the pupil record sheets can vary, but a style should be agreed by teachers, as they will be passed from year to year and inconsistent practice will make the record less useful.

Brief comments should note why a pupil's progress has been slow or rapid, e.g. through absence, lack of interest or motivation, etc., and note if any evidence has been retained in the school portfolio for this particular child.

Benefits of this system

■ Teachers can see at a glance the general progress being made by a class. Particular difficulties can be quickly identified.

■ Teachers can easily refer to particular explanations for unexpected issues and problems.

■ It makes possible a simple measure of 'value added', in that the class record can show a move from average to more rapid progress (or vice versa).

■ The sheets can facilitate the compilation of reports. The individual pupil record sheet can highlight particular points it may be desirable to include in annual reports.

■ Information can be passed on from teacher to teacher. Because the sheets are not restricted to a single year, some measure of progress can be determined.

■ Any teacher receiving these sheets can see at a glance the main developments of the class and particular issues for pupils.

■ The information can be used formatively and diagnostically. Explanations are offered for particular instances of progress and teachers should be able to isolate the main issues and act on them accordingly.

STAGE 7: PREPARING A RESOURCE BOX

This stage should run alongside Stages 1–6.

No matter how experienced teachers may be, there are likely to be difficulties if they work in isolation. Benchmarks are often needed to establish standards against which to assess. Exemplar material will be a crucial part of the standardising process. Many primary schools are already preparing a series of resource boxes for curriculum areas (see pages 44–45). These should also contain assessment material such as:

1 sample tasks;

2 examples of pupil work which show performance at the three levels (green, orange and red) noted on the class record sheet, ideally with annotations and comments explaining what makes each standard (see the three samples of work on evacuation in Figure 3.4 A–C on pages 65–67.

3 examples of good practice in marking pupil work. OFSTED and others have criticised marking practice in history. In their report on history in 1992–93, OFSTED stated that clear guidance was seldom given on how pupils might improve performance, marking was often too generalised and the focus was predominantly on linguistic rather than historical capabilities.

(Examples of good practice in these three categories can be gathered gradually and could include contributions from different teachers).

4 some guidance on particular features associated with progress made in history. Two photocopiable examples are included at 3.8 and 3.9 below.

The first (pages 69–70) gives examples of how you might define levels within your own assessment objectives for history. You might not feel this is necessary, but if you do then such data should be attached to exemplar tasks.

The second (page 71) is an attempt to define the kind of variables that you should be looking for in historical skills. These cut across or overarch the assessment objectives which are much more specific to the areas defined by the attainment target.

You might also look closely at the section headed Historical Investigation (Key Elements 4a, 4b and 4c) in Section 2.

Figure 3.2

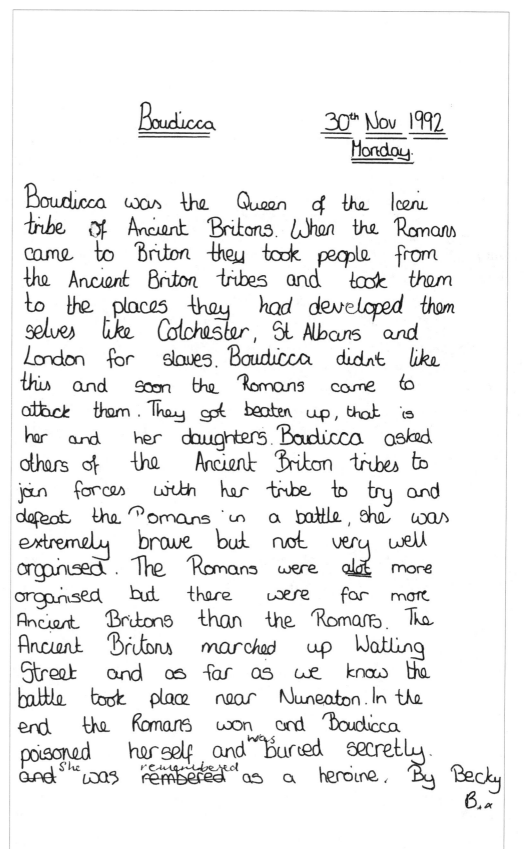

Boudicca   30th Nov 1992
                              Monday.

Boudicca was the Queen of the Iceni tribe of Ancient Britons. When the Romans came to Briton they took people from the Ancient Briton tribes and took them to the places they had developed them selves like Colchester, St Albans and London for slaves. Boudicca didn't like this and soon the Romans came to attack them. They got beaten up, that is her and her daughters. Boudicca asked others of the Ancient Briton tribes to join forces with her tribe to try and defeat the Romans in a battle, she was extremely brave but not very well organised. The Romans were alot more organised but there were far more Ancient Britons than the Romans. The Ancient Britons marched up Watling Street and as far as we know the battle took place near Nuneaton. In the end the Romans won and Boudicca poisoned herself and was buried secretly. and she was remembered as a heroine. By Becky B.x

EXAMPLE 3.6: ANALYSING PUPILS' WORK ON CAUSATION/MOTIVATION IN KEY STAGE 2

Figure 3.2 (page 63) is an account of Boudicca's defeat by the Romans. The pupils had heard and read the story. They then had to write a brief account explaining why Boudicca rebelled and also why the Romans won and Boudicca lost. The Year 5/Year 6 class were asked to produce an extended piece of writing covering these issues. The example is by a Year 5 pupil.

Commentary (on Boudicca)
This account is fairly well written. It follows a logical order and the pupil's grasp of events is sound. She is aware of the main places and the nature of the two protagonists. The issue of causation is addressed explicitly. She addresses the two specific aspects she has been asked to focus on – the causes of the revolt and the reasons for the outcome.

However, although the teacher encouraged pupils to look for more than one reason for the events, this pupil has largely contented herself with a single reason for the revolt, i.e. the poor treatment by the Romans of the native Britons including Boudicca. The outcome is explained by the better organisation of the Romans. The teacher had gone to some length to cover other reasons for the revolt and the way that the Romans and Iceni responded to events. Some attention had also been given to various choices available to both sides. The teacher also wanted pupils to dwell on the effects of the revolt, which had been covered in the class. This pupil largely restricted herself to what happened to Boudicca alone. Even so, this is a creditable piece of work showing that she has a grasp of what causes are and can use valid, if limited, reasons to explain why things turned out as they did.

Figure 3.3 is a piece of work on the Spanish Armada. The pupils had been studying the events associated with the Spanish Armada. They had covered the reasons why the Armada came, the way the Spanish

Figure 3.3

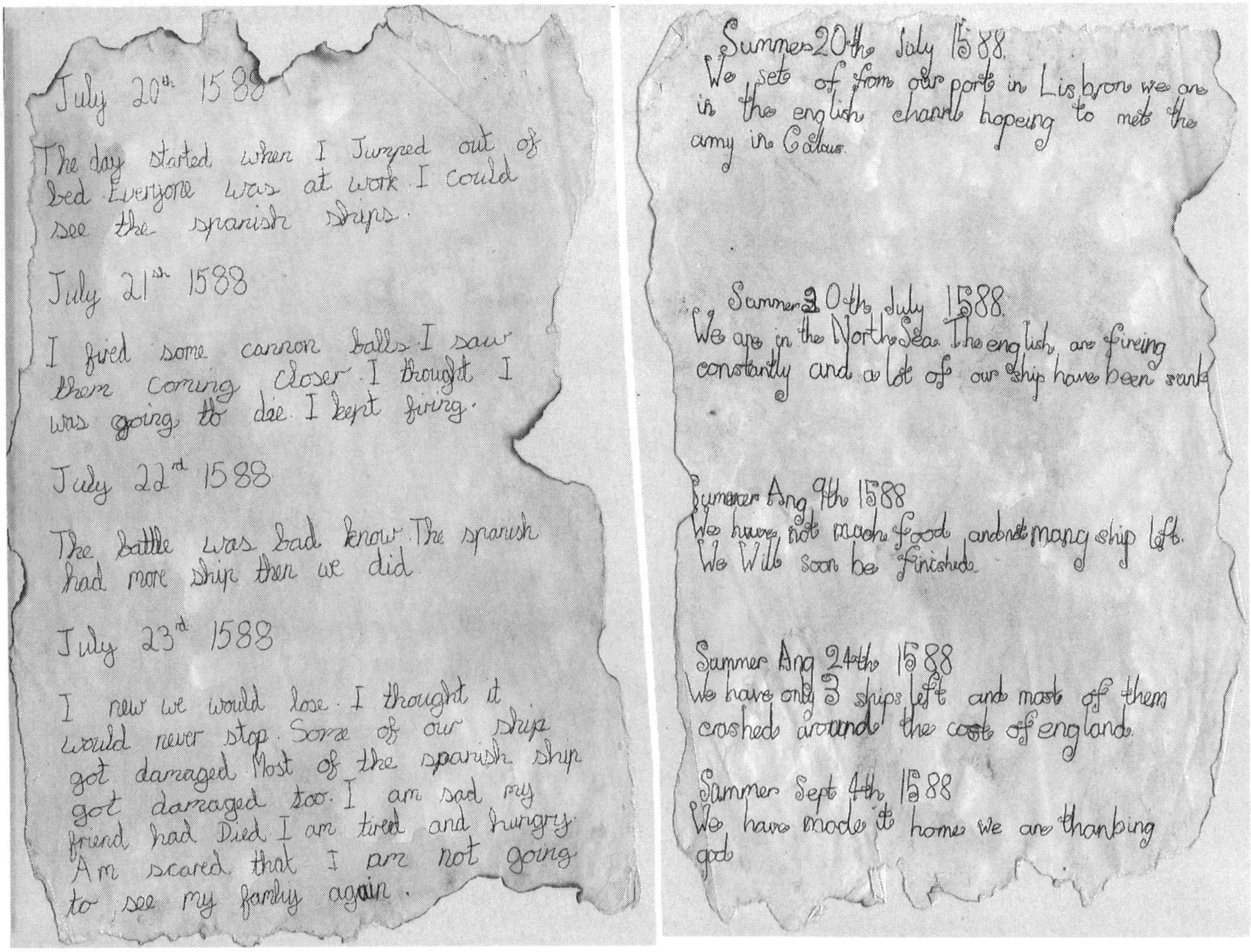

July 20th 1588

The day started when I Jumped out of bed. Everyone was at work. I could see the spanish ships.

July 21st 1588

I fired some cannon balls. I saw them coming closer. I thought I was going to die. I kept firing.

July 22nd 1588

The battle was bad know. The spanish had more ship then we did.

July 23rd 1588

I new we would lose. I thought it would never stop. Some of our ship got damaged. Most of the spanish ship got damaged too. I am sad my friend had Died. I am tired and hungry. Am scared that I am not going to see my famly again.

Summer 20th July 1588.

We sets of from our port in Lisbon we are in the english channle hopeing to meet the amy in Calais.

Summer 30th July 1588.

We are in the North Sea. The english are fireing constantly and a lot of our ship have been sank.

Summer Aug 9th 1588

We have not much food and not many ship left. We Will soon be finished.

Summer Aug 24th 1588

We have only 3 ships left and most of them crashed around the cost of england.

Summer Sept 4th 1588

We have made it home we are thanking god.

expected to win the battle, and the reasons for the defeat. The teacher then asked pupils to write a diary entry for each of the two sides. The aim was for the diaries to explain why events turned out as they did. The example is from a Year 4 pupil.

Commentary (on Spanish Armada)

Clearly, the pupil has enjoyed the activity and done what is commonplace in schools – simulating contemporary documents. However, an analysis of the historical content reveals very little reference to reasons, choices and outcomes. Little attention is given to the issues of the time. It comes across as a fairly low level account of the events, with descriptions which could apply to almost any period of history, e.g. I jumped out of bed; I am tired and hungry. The activity does not provide sufficient evidence that the pupil has a real feel for the events. The descriptions are rather wooden. The failure of the pupil to identify reasons for the defeat of the Armada may be the fault of the task as much as of the pupil. However, the pupil has given no real thought to the reasons for the turn of events. It would perhaps have been better if the teacher had used an alternative task in which the causation questions could have been made more central.

EXAMPLE 3.7: PUPILS' WORK ON THE SECOND WORLD WAR

Background

The pupils were from a class containing Year 5 and Year 6 pupils. They had been studying the topic of Britain since 1930. They had previously studied photographic evidence, read a fictional account and discussed the process of evacuation and why it took place, as well as the attitudes and feelings that people must have had about it.

Pupils were then asked to do a piece of writing describing the experience of evacuation. It was to be written as if the pupil were the person being evacuated. It had to describe both the details of the evacuation and the feelings of the people affected by it.

Figure 3.4
Sample A

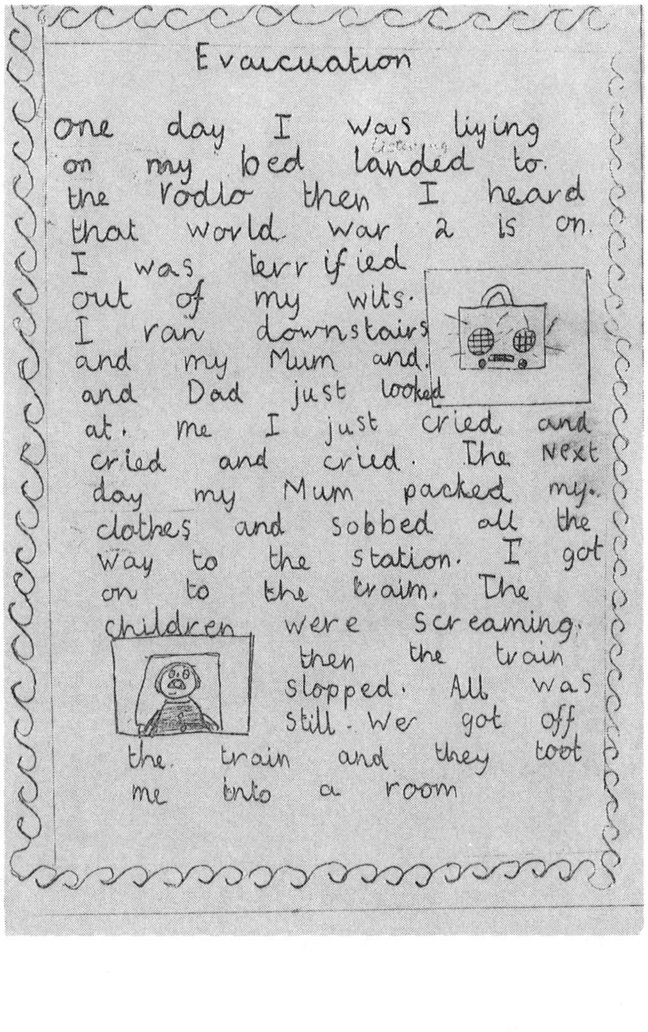

Evacuation

One day I was lying on my bed landed to the rodio then I heard that world war 2 is on. I was terrified out of my wits. I ran downstairs and my Mum and and Dad just looked at me I just cried and cried and cried. The Next day my Mum packed my clothes and sobbed all the way to the station. I got on to the train. The children were screaming. then the train stopped. All was still. We got off the train and they toot me into a room

Sample B

Evacuation   Sam

I am Barry Durose, aged 10. I am 11 on the 5th November. I was born in 1929. I live at 16 Old Kent Road. We are not a very wealthy family. My Dad is in the army. My Mum works at a clothes factory on Fleet Street.

September 1st 1939 Saturday

I got up at 9.30. I turned the radio I listened to some jazz by Glenn Miller. Then I got washed and dressed in my. Long Johns, Jumper, Cap, pants and socks. I then went down stairs. I heard Mum and Dad talking about me and my sister going away. I felt excited, speachless, flabbergasted, and happy. I was in a good mood for the rest of the morning. In the afternoon I went to fetch the Sunday Times for Dad. On the way home I read the back page Everton had beaten Nottingham Forest 5-0 Dixie

Dean had scored 3 and Tom Browel Then I noticed the front page. CHILDREN GO AWAY WHILE WARS ON. I thought about Dad talking about me and my sister going away When I got home I went to bed because it was 5.30 pm

September 2nd 1939 Sunday

I got up excited, I was playing for my team at football Unborugh Grammer. My Dads taking us in our Austin 100 1.1 We got there about 10.00am. We got ready we went out on the pitch. I said hello to our star striker who's scored 45 goals in 16 games, he brill. We were playing Colly Grammer who were top. It was nearly half time when I yes me scored a great goal with my head like Dixie Dean my favourite player. At the end It was 1-0 to us YEEEE!!! When we got home Mum and Dad had a talk with me and my sister.

We were going away about 200 miles !!! I felt terrified and my sister started crying I was ashamed of her because she to 14 !!! I went to bed at 5.45 pm I started sobbing on my pillow. Fortunately Dad heard me and had a talk about it. "It was the safest thing. because of the war" Dad said "so" "what" I interrupted "a war you'll be in it" Dad then went out of the room.

September 3rd 1939 Monday

I got up at 12-noon Mum was packing my bag, I felt so depressed. I feel I could kill Hitler. I think about my Dad going in that bloody war. She packs me some food. We had a phonecall at 9.42 about going to school at 1.00pm it was now 12.30pm. When the bag was packed we went downstairs and had a talk about old times, it was so depressing. The old clock struck 1.00pm. Mum and Dad

took me to school. We lined up in single file we walked to the station and got on the train. I started crying and waved a last goodbye. The train started moving. My Mum started crying and ran after me but she couldn't catch up. The train journey went into the night. I went to sleep sorrowful and dejected.

September 4th 1939 Tuesday

When I woke up we were nearly there. When we got there we went into a hall, I looked around there were alot of old women. Paul said "Were being picked" "Picked for what" I replied. "Where were going to live" he said I paused, I then remember what dad had said. My best mate Paul was picked by a quite young person. It was time for me to be picked I was picked by a grumpy old woman. I felt so dismal!

Sample C

Being Evacuated

It all came upon me when I was having breakfast when my Mum said, come along it's time for school' She sounded really unhappy. So I did as I was told and went to school ") felt really miserable When I got to school I was told to go back home and pack. I felt so unhappy I went running up stairs I cried and cried." Just then my mother said "come on down stairs" i walked slowly down stairs really miserable, and my mother says "don't worry about leaving home I will come and see you soon "But I don't want to leave you" "I'm sorry about not telling you there is a war on but mum why didn't you tell me before" "Darling I would have but your father told me to keep it quiet otherwise I would have told you" So my mother went up stairs help me pack a case. We were to go to line up Then the teacher said "Say goodbye and get on the train. So we all got on the train. We all waved goodbye.

We was all crying about leaving our parents. We all were very sad. When the train stopped we all had some food when we had finished the train started again and off we went, all very miserabley and very unhappy.

When the train had reached Wales we had to go in a hall and line up and wait for someone to pick us. We were all crying. untill along comes the teacher and says "please stop crying" so we all tried but it was hard Then some comes up to me and says "I know why you are crying don't woory I want to take you home with me"

Lindsey

Comments

It would be generally accepted that Sample A was the weakest and Sample B the best account.

In part, this is due to the quality of language and organisation. This should not be totally ignored when assessing the historical quality of a piece of work, as history is, at least in part, a literary subject.

However, there are also clear historical criteria.

Sample B

Sample B (page 66) clearly shows a better grasp of the historical context. A better understanding of historical knowledge is demonstrated. This knowledge (based partly on research) is used to good effect. For example, the pupil chooses a realistic area for the evacuee; the detail about his music and football are realistically portrayed; the dates are accurate. Such details are woven effectively into the account of feeling and attitudes.

There are times when the pupil's love of football almost seems to get the better of the account. There are also some anachronisms – it is possible that the family had a telephone, but unlikely. Nevertheless, the piece conveys well the mixed emotions likely to be felt by families and demonstrates knowledge of the organisation of evacuation.

Sample C

Some of this feeling also comes over in Sample C above – the distress felt by parents and the ignorance shown by many children.

However, the previous work done on the topic has not been incorporated effectively into the account. It does refer to the role of schools, travel to places such as Wales on trains and the process of evacuation. In general though it is rather limited on historical detail. Unlike Sample B, there has been little attempt to convey a particular sense of atmosphere with reference to sport, music, etc. By and large it would be possible to get to the beginning of the last paragraph without realising that this was an account about evacuation. It could almost refer to a present-day school residential visit, with a child going away from home for the first time.

Sample A

This is even more true of Sample A (page 65). It does convey some of the atmosphere of someone upset about leaving home. However, apart from a couple of isolated references, e.g. to the fact that it was the radio being listened to and that the evacuation followed soon after the start of the War, it could almost refer to any period of history. It is also very thin on historical detail.

Despite that, it is almost as good as Sample C in reflecting valid attitudes – fear, uncertainty, the distress of the mother. However, these can be viewed as normal feelings for any people in such circumstances. They have not been well linked to that particular period of history.

EXAMPLE 3.8: POSSIBLE PERFORMANCES AGAINST THE OBJECTIVES

■ Assessment Objective 1
Example 1
Lower: Can sequence one or two objects related to everyday life, e.g. kitchen equipment, costumes, houses where the differences are distinct.
Middle: Can sequence events in a story or a person's life, possibly making use of jumbled cards.
Upper: Can investigate an event, a theme or a person's life, selecting material and presenting the main features on a timeline.

Example 2
Lower: Can use a limited number of time terms, such as 'today', 'yesterday', 'now', 'then', 'old', 'new', and talk about everyday life accurately using these terms.
Middle: Can refer to time terms showing the passage of time, e.g. 'decades', 'centuries', as well as to period labels such as 'Roman', 'Victorian'.
Upper: Can produce accounts incorporating dates accurately including, where appropriate, BC and AD.

Example 3
Lower: Can group categories of historical objects, e.g. coins, toys, weapons, furniture.
Middle: Can compare and contrast straightforward differences in lifestyles within the same period of history, e.g. the lives of people in Athens and Sparta.
Upper: Can recall previously learnt information to compare the lives of people or events from other study units covered, e.g. family life in two different periods.

■ Assessment Objective 2
Example 1
Lower: Knows about a few of the features associated with the study unit, e.g. people, events, situations.
Middle: Can talk about a period of history referring to some of the variety of lifestyles, e.g. rich and poor, children and adults.
Upper: Can write about different people in a study unit and comment about what these people may have felt about their situations.

Example 2
Lower: Not appropriate.
Middle: Can use one or two of the listed terms in a single context, e.g. court.
Upper: Can recognise more than one characteristic of the same historical term or feature, e.g. how the term 'industry' might mean different things in Saxon and Victorian England.

■ Assessment Objective 3
Lower: Can spot some differences between pictures of the same place, e.g. a street scene, at two different periods, producing a reason why one or two things have changed.
Middle: Can identify two or three reasons for an action or two or three things that have happened as a result of that action, perhaps using a book.
Upper: Can offer some comments on which reasons may be the more important in explaining an event or why major changes have occurred, e.g. why the Armada was defeated.

■ **Assessment Objective 4**
Lower: Can listen to two stories of a life or select pictures to go with a statement made, e.g. about a child's unhappiness in a Victorian school.
Middle: Chooses aspects of the same event from two commercial schemes and selects and identifies differences, e.g. working children in Victorian families.
Upper: Can present a viewpoint and rewrite from another point of view.

■ **Assessment Objective 5**
Lower: Teachers pose a limited number of questions and pupils locate information from a source or a limited number of sources.
Middle: Using a mix of teacher-generated and pupil-devised questions, pupils can find answers from a limited range of source material. When prompted by the teacher, can make straightforward comments on the usefulness of sources.
Upper: Pupils can, largely, devise a series of questions; can then locate and communicate answers by using a range of different sources including some complex ones. Can also offer some pertinent comments on the usefulness of the material, e.g. problems of reliability.

■ **Assessment Objective 6**
Example 1
Lower: Can choose one or two pieces of information from a site to answer a historical question, e.g. How easy was it to cook in a castle long ago? How cold was it for people?
Middle: Can select material provided by the teacher to deal with a small historical investigation and then write a paragraph answering a question, e.g. What happened to Boudicca?
Upper: Can produce a wall display or 'group book' based on the location and organisation of a range of material, e.g. about life for different people in the Tudor countryside.

Example 2
Lower: Can reply orally to a question posed by the teacher, e.g. What kind of games did your grandparents like to play?
Middle: Can write an accurate paragraph in response to a question asked by the teacher, e.g. How did Henry VIII manage to upset the Roman Catholic Church?
Upper: Following an investigation, a group of pupils can present their findings using different forms of communication, e.g. extended writing, information technology, pictures and drawings, role plays, on a topic such as 'What was it like to live through the Blitz?'

EXAMPLE 3.9: SOME QUESTIONS TO ASK ABOUT PUPILS' PROGRESS IN HISTORY

1 **Are the pupils being more selective when answering historical questions,** e.g. can they choose relevant and significant information from the sources?

2 **Can they use concepts more confidently,** e.g. general concepts such as change and cause as well as specific terms such as 'parliament', 'monarch'?

3 **Can they use their imagination and common sense in an increasingly mature way when carrying out history tasks,** e.g. imagining what people must have felt at a particular time; making deductions about what happened; sorting out disparate information; extracting maximum potential from sources?

4 **Can pupils show greater skill at making connections, comparisons and contrasts when carrying out history tasks,** e.g. weaving together different and seemingly disconnected aspects; comparing and contrasting information across time, geographical areas, perspectives and dimensions such as political, social and gender? Also, can they develop better skills at showing how typical something was?

5 **Can they just describe or are they improving their competence at explaining things, such as why events turned out as they did?**

6 **Can they summarise the key features about historical people, events and situations whilst also showing a greater database of historical information?**

7 **Are they becoming better at planning, organising and communicating history,** e.g. showing more independence and initiative with aspects such as order, balance, accuracy, logic, objectivity, knowing what to omit; using and evaluating sources; providing clear and uncluttered information; posing good questions and then working out how to answer them; making sensible inferences; producing logical, relevant and accurate communication?

8 **Do they show an increasing awareness of the uncertainty of history,** e.g. avoiding sweeping assertions and becoming more tentative and sceptical?

STAGE 8: PUPIL SELF-ASSESSMENT

This is an optional stage which can complement the teacher's own assessment.

There are benefits to be gained from both pupil self-assessment and some assessment by peers of other work done in the class. There are clearly time implications and doubts about reliability. However, it is an approach worth considering – perhaps at the end of each study unit.

For example, pupils might be asked to fill in answers to the following questions for each study unit:

■ What have you most enjoyed about this topic?

■ What have you least enjoyed about this topic?

■ Are there any parts you found boring?

■ What do you feel has been the most useful thing you have learnt about this topic?

■ Write down which parts you found difficult or did not do very well in.

■ Write down any parts you feel you did very well in.

■ Are there any ways you would want to see this topic changed if you were doing it again?

Once they have completed the form, the teacher might find time to speak briefly to each pupil to discuss an aspect of history he or she could do

Figure 3.5

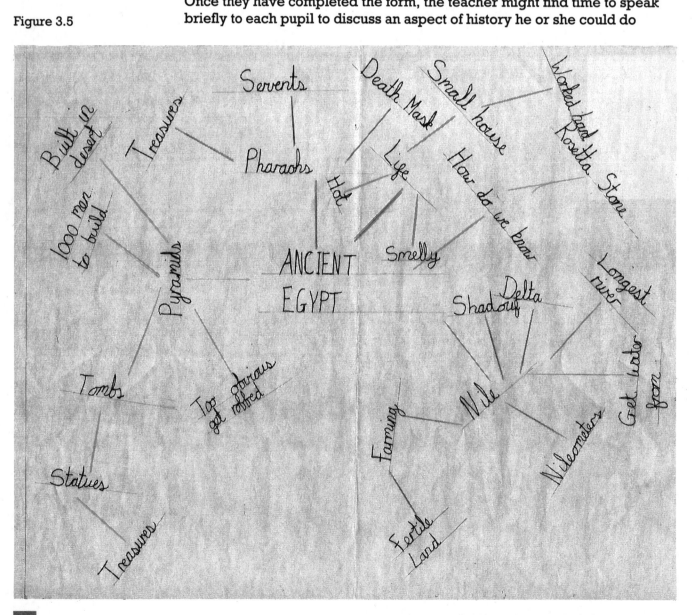

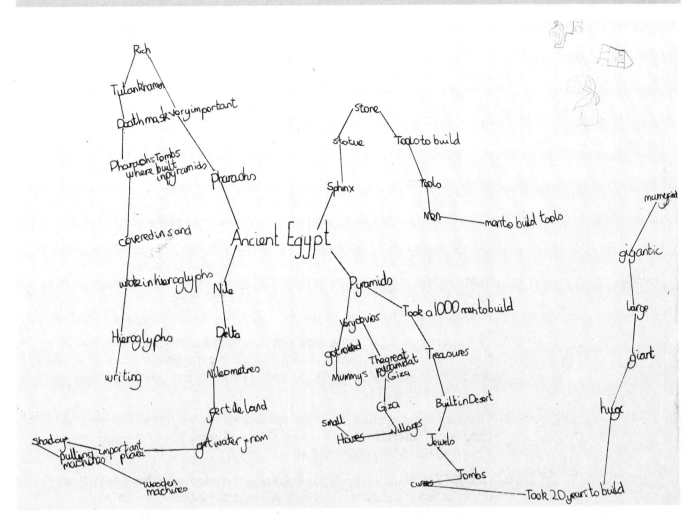

Figure 3.6

better next time. It might be a general skill, such as presentation, or a specific historical skill, such as using more dates in his or her writing. These evaluations could be filed and brought out during the study of the next unit so that pupils could be reminded of the 'targets' set.

Such evaluations are suitable for older pupils in Key Stage 2. Although first attempts at such evaluations are generally poor, teachers report that most pupils gradually improve and become more objective and specific.

The advantages of carrying out these evaluations in moderation are:

■ it can increase pupils' confidence and hopefully their motivation;

■ it can make them more aware of assessment criteria;

■ it can give teachers some idea of the effectiveness of aspects of the teaching and learning programme;

■ it can create a dialogue between teacher and pupils;

■ it can act as a form of revision and a way to round off units.

An alternative approach which serves a slightly different purpose is to ask pupils to complete a flow diagram recalling and connecting what they have covered in a topic. This allows the teacher to gain a general grasp of a pupil's knowledge and understanding. Figures 3.5 and 3.6 are examples of such an exercise done by pupils in a school following completion of work on Ancient Egypt.

STAGE 9: MAINTAINING CONSISTENT STANDARDS

Central to any effective assessment scheme is the need for teachers to understand as fully as possible what differentiates good from less good history work. It goes without saying that it is pointless setting the world's best tasks if teachers cannot distinguish a good from a bad answer when they see one.

As so many teachers are not history specialists, it is advisable to try to ensure that there is a common understanding of standards. The previous steps provide some checks and guidance; the following may be valid forms of monitoring to help standardisation.

1 Occasional staff meetings could be held to calibrate examples of pupils' work – possibly examples taken from the resource box or about to be added to it. All existing annotations would be erased. Teachers would then discuss the standards. This would help the standardisation process, as well as keeping relevant assessment criteria to the fore.

2 Similar calibration meetings might be held with teachers in other schools. This would help provide some standardisation across schools. There could also be benefit from occasional meetings with local secondary schools to allow discussion of progression in history across phases.

3 The coordinator could devote some time to looking at examples of history done in different classes, examining the coverage, the nature of the tasks, marking, recording sheets, reports, etc. Ideally, feedback would be provided.

4 The coordinator and/or a senior member of staff might analyse the results obtained from different classes. Any trends or discrepancies would need to be probed further.

5 *Limited* evidence could be retained to indicate how the school has interpreted standards. Only a small number of samples of work representing different standards would be needed. At most, it might mean a single portfolio, including examples from each class, as a check on internal consistency. At best, if there is a system of calibration of work as described above, it may be necessary to do no more than keep a general sample of work covering the range of achievements and assessment objectives for each year for history. These retained examples would provide a series of 'benchmarks' to:

■ influence marking by individual teachers;

■ demonstrate to others, such as OFSTED, where the school has pitched its marking in history.

The evidence should be reviewed on occasion, and out-of-date pieces replaced with clearer 'benchmark' examples suitably annotated to demonstrate the standard and the reason for the way in which it has been assessed.

STAGE 10: KEEPING YOUR SYSTEM IN GOOD REPAIR

The evidence provided by this system should be monitored at least annually to determine:

■ the reliability of assessment tasks;

■ the difficulty and simplicity of aspects of the teaching programme;

■ pupils' interest and motivation;

■ the rate of progress;

■ standards in relation to pupils of similar ages and abilities;

■ the effectiveness of approaches to differentiation.

When it comes to reconsidering future activities, the evaluation of the previous records should play a major part in influencing the programme.

Also critically important is the feedback from the other people who need to use this information – other teachers, different schools, coordinators, senior management, those doing appraisal, OFSTED, parents, governors. They need something accessible, meaningful, relevant and reliable.

There is one other group of people who probably need the assessment information even more than those listed above – the pupils themselves. Most existing schemes ignore this. If improved pupil learning is to be one of the central objectives of a good recording scheme, it is obviously necessary for pupils to be aware of the progress they are making – which takes us on to Stage 11.

STAGE 11: REPORTING Reports should:

■ refer to what has been learned as well as taught;

■ relate to National Curriculum achievement, ideally referring to specific content and pieces of work – they should not be so general that it is impossible to see what subject area is being reported on;

■ be relatively brief and jargon-free so that parents and children can use them – they should never be ambiguous or in a kind of secret code;

■ consist of more than unexplained grades;

■ be a fair reflection of achievement and not give a distorted impression of what the pupil has done or not done – they may well emphasise positive achievement but weaknesses should not be ignored;

■ aim to motivate by indicating any suggestions for improvement: any targets should be realistic and comprehensible to pupils;

■ adopt the framework common to the school;

■ allow parents an opportunity to respond – preferably serving as a complement to parents' meetings;

■ conform to statutory requirements, i.e. noting achievement against level descriptions at the end of Years 2 and 6, when and if implemented after 1995; producing comments on progress in history at least annually.

Approaches to the study units

4.1 Key Stage 1 history

It would be easy to dismiss history in Key Stage 1. There are a number of reasons for this. Many argue that this is really a time to concentrate on the basics of reading, writing and number work. Others argue that this is not the time for pupils to start thinking about history, as they are not up to it. If anything, this is a 'pre-history' period. The odd reference to the past can be comfortably incorporated into a general topic approach. After all, the flexibility and freedom provided by the friendly Orders helps achieve this. There is little specific content. Moreover, recent reports and surveys suggest that the quality of teaching and learning is generally fine at this key stage and that the relative paucity of complaints from teachers has produced an optimistic air.

Whilst there is much to be pleased about, there is no room for complacency. A recent OFSTED survey (1992–93) found standards higher than in other key stages (80 per cent of lessons were satisfactory or better), that they were particularly good in reception classes and that teaching and learning were approximately of the same standard.

However, the same survey has drawn attention to less impressive aspects of Key Stage 1 history, such as lack of clear objectives, a poor match of tasks to pupils' capabilities, the setting of low-level tasks such as copying and colouring in, limited assessment and limited resources. It also pointed out that relatively few schools had reviewed topics to ensure that all the Key Stage 1 requirements had been adequately covered.

Problems and strategies

One school's approach to the establishing of a good Key Stage 1 history programme is outlined below.

EXAMPLE 4.1: DIFFICULTIES AND OPPORTUNITIES

The coordinator in the school had attended a number of courses. Following this, she was asked to lead a staff meeting in which the teachers first of all brainstormed all the difficulties they saw with teaching Key Stage 1 history. Once that had been done, they outlined the teaching opportunities which existed. It was felt that the parameters had to be defined in this way before considering the topics, which was the next step. What they came up with is described below.

Difficulties
1 Trying to teach appropriate history to pupils as young as four.
2 Inadequate resources (or at least those we know about).

3 The need to cover so much else and pressure to focus on the three Rs.

4 The limited ability of such young children to understand and grasp history. For example:

■ Most pupils in Key Stage 1 see the past as amorphous.

■ Their grasp of terms is different from that of adults, even terms such as 'king', 'queen', 'palace'.

■ They can begin to sequence but in a limited way. Many pupils even at the end of Key Stage 1 are just coming to terms with 'oldest', 'middle' and 'youngest'. In any case, we find that sequencing is not a natural skill for pupils. Sequence requires some logic and we find pupils require experience for this. Another basic difficulty is that they find the idea of 'beginning' very difficult.

■ Their grasp of numbers also affects their ability to cope with the concept of time. Five-year-old pupils have little concept of numbers beyond 100. Most dates contain four digits and even our nine-year-old pupils find this difficult.

■ The pupils' grasp of the idea of change seems limited throughout Key Stage 1. Even older pupils see change largely in terms of direct actions performed and the substitution of one thing for another. They cannot fit it into a time frame. They are, at best, often restricted to the idea of similarity and difference.

■ Their restricted language and reading and writing skills affect their progress in history. Any investigations are inevitably limited. They also have problems using written sources which is a Key Stage 1 requirement.

■ They find it difficult to distinguish the real from the fictional. Where stories seem realistic, such as in the legend of King Arthur, most could not distinguish reality from fiction.

■ They have a limited grasp of sources. At best they can extract limited information from them, but they have no real grasp of their context. They also have a distorted view about many sources. For example, they find it difficult to distinguish the age of a pictorial source from the ages of the people depicted in the sources; they think of black and white pictures as automatically older than colour ones; they equate shiny artefacts with newness and broken and dusty ones with age.

■ They find it difficult to relate to particular types of character. They seem to relate to 'naughty' people much better than to others. Their relative inexperience of life prevents them from relating to adults and adult values. They also seem to find it difficult to relate to children from the past, or to children in stories who are mature for their years.

■ Many of the resources give a distorted image. For example, some of the best-loved children's stories portray blonde princesses needing help from brave, handsome, white princes. Also, old age and blackness are associated with evil.

■ Many children, even at the age of seven, lack the social skills to cope with group work.

■ We like to use content which the pupils can relate to. This means a heavy stress on self and family. However, we have many children who are not from traditional nuclear families or who have 'skeletons in the cupboard' and this causes insurmountable problems. If nothing else, it means we cannot use such families or expect these children to ask their parents and grandparents to fill in questionnaires.

■ Pupils seem to acquire historical skills so slowly that we need to reinforce things constantly.

What can we get pupils to do and understand?

Our experience suggests that, with careful preparation and targeting, pupils can:

■ tell and re-tell a story;

■ have some grasp of the feelings of others and the simple motives of people – they seem to be able to grasp motives before causes and many by the age of seven can make comments about the actions and thoughts of other people;

■ draw some conclusions about sources, e.g. seven-year-old pupils can make simple deductions about an artefact;

■ ask as well as answer simple questions;

■ suggest similarities and differences, especially regarding places and periods (e.g. here/there and then/now), as long as they are quite distinct;

■ demonstrate some referencing skills, e.g. finding basic information in topic books, from a simple written source or from an artefact;

■ distinguish photographs from pictures;

■ observe features in pictorial sources – by the age of seven they can note minute details even if they find it difficult to detect patterns;

■ carry out activities related to artefacts such as drawing, labelling, measuring, colouring, weighing, feeling, commenting on their use and value;

■ produce personal timelines showing four or five key events in a time relationship by the age of six;

■ sequence three or four events in a story or artefacts by this age;

■ begin to cope with simple family trees (although not the dates) by the age of seven;

■ use a number of time words such as 'today', 'tomorrow', the days of the week, months and seasons;

■ compare similarities and differences in situations, people and events;

■ a few pupils by the age of seven are surprisingly good at making sense of sources, even in their original format.

Looking at Key Stage 1 as a whole

The next stage in the school's planning was to look at the key stage as a whole. Although the coordinator played the leading role, all teachers were asked to contribute and offer constructive comment. They felt there were four whole Key Stage 1 issues to address before individual topics were considered:

1   What types of topic might encourage a history emphasis and the development of historical skills and concepts?

2   What specific terms and concepts should we try to get over to pupils and reinforce through regular use?

3   What types of source might we want to use with pupils of this age?

4   Are there any key ideas we would want to get over to pupils and reinforce during the key stage (and into Key Stage 2 and beyond)?

Clearly, the National Curriculum requirements helped define the answers but, although teachers were generally aware of these, they did not act as a check until the four questions had been brainstormed.

TOPICS

'What types of topic might encourage a history emphasis and the development of historical skills and concepts?'

The following seem to offer rich potential for developing history:

1 **Myself and my family** (see the example on pages 86–90).

2 **Homes** (this can be linked to Key Stage 2) – different types of homes, surveys; rooms in houses and their functions; sequence types of homes; discuss features; interview relatives and others about homes in their youth; discuss similarities and differences and how and why things have changed; look at pictures and photographs of homes in the past showing aspects such as heating, lighting and cleaning and the ways things are different, e.g. cooking, vacuum cleaners, electric lighting; look at censuses for clues about houses in the past, e.g. servants and large families; use stories; visit an old house (or rooms) in a museum; homes of different types in different times and cultures, e.g. a Roman villa, castles, stately homes, caves; stories; role play, e.g. as servants in a Victorian house; gender roles in homes in the past; stories of events told from the viewpoint of the house over a long period of time; pupils distinguish realistic from fictional stories of houses, e.g. an eyewitness account of a Victorian household and *Toad of Toad Hall*; match artefacts to rooms.

3 **Journeys** – surveys on where we travel to, e.g. school, shops, holidays; how we get there and how long it takes; how the journeys have changed, e.g. locations, methods of transport, time taken; whether some things have remained the same; maps and plans showing some journeys using symbols; stories of conditions and dangers on journeys in the past, e.g. sea voyages, stage coaches, early railways, early flight; stories of one or two pioneers and improvers, e.g. Telford, Blind Jack of Knaresborough, early explorers, female travellers, Trevithick, the Wright Brothers; journeys through time involving timelines, stories and research dealing with lifestyles for the time destination.

4 **People and work** – jobs people do, e.g. milkman, shopkeeper, teacher, transport worker; interview people who do these jobs; find out about such jobs in the past, e.g. through pictures, stories, reference books, interviews; directories can list trades in the locality; look at advertisements; make lists of similarities and differences; jobs done by women; stories of jobs done by people in the past and which no longer exist, e.g. in castles, in travel, stage coach owner, music hall, a king or queen – why jobs have changed; possibly discuss fact and fiction; clothes worn by people doing jobs now and in the past; jobs to do with history, e.g. museum curator – see work and make own museum with labels back in classroom.

5 **Our local area** – what the main buildings are; what they are called; try to place them on maps or aerial photographs; look at simple changes on maps and diagrams – whether names have changed; what the names mean; who gave them the names; stories of people who gave names, e.g. Vikings, Victorians; changing functions; clues about buildings and their uses, e.g. dates, styles, names; categorise buildings according to age and type; sequence designs, e.g. windows, doors; compare street scenes at 100-year intervals – what is similar and what is different, what is better and what is worse; why uses have changed; who used buildings in the past; role play historical events in a local building, e.g. a fire; use censuses, directories, pictures, photographs, interviews with

relatives and others, a local trail; what is worth preserving in the area; look for evidence of 'mock designs'.

6 **Shops and shopping** – why we use shops, what happens in shops, the use of money; shops in the past and differences from the present, e.g. small shops, packaging; what shops existed in the area in the past; what they sold; role play a shopping trip; make shopping lists and compare past and present; interview relatives and others about shops and shopping; use censuses and directories, pictures, photographs, visits to a museum, various documents such as advertisements, receipts and bills; set up the home corner as an old-fashioned corner shop, e.g. with old scales, own packaging, bottles, boxes, coins.

7 **Festivals and celebrations** – what we celebrate personally and in the family, e.g. birthdays, Christmas; other types of celebration, e.g. Guy Fawkes, Olympic Games, Poppy Day, harvest festival; celebrations and festivals of different religions, cultures and regions; local celebrations such as Furry Dances and May Day; use sources to see how these have changed, e.g. Victorian Christmas from pictures, old cards, fictional story, eyewitness accounts; role play.

8 **Seasons** – things that happen in particular seasons; make timelines, e.g. Christmas, Diwali and other festivals, holidays, Guy Fawkes, local events; investigate, e.g. using books and talking to older people, how things were different in the past; make lists of similarities and differences; clothes in different seasons and how these have changed in the past; seasons in other countries and times and stories of people involved, e.g. flooding in Ancient Egypt; travel in winter on old roads; holidays now and then; poems and music associated with different seasons – link music to different times; problems in the past caused by seasons, e.g. farming, travel, heating and lighting, shortage of food, flooding, e.g. 1953 floods.

9 **Childhood** – changes in lifestyle, clothes, toys and games; schools in own, parents' and grandparents' time; stories of childhood at times in the past, e.g. evacuation, child labour, Victorian schools; visit to a reconstructed schoolroom or a museum of childhood depicting Victorian times; sources can include artefacts, visits, use of school log books, buildings, pictures and photographs, nursery rhymes and childhood songs, oral history from relations and others.

10 **Grannies and grandads** – favourite things about grandparents; simple family trees; explain how names often change on marriage; talk to grandparents about their lives, hobbies, holidays and houses when they were the ages of the pupils; survey how many had televisions when they were young; observe pictures and films of life when grandparents were young; examine artefacts used and compare with modern equivalents; talk about their beliefs, treasured possessions and concerns; look at the experiences of grandparents, contrasting their upbringing and perhaps using stories, e.g. P. Heaslip, *Grandma's Favourites* (mixed races), *Katie Morag and the Two Grandmothers*; stories about grandparents to show they were young once, e.g. E. Janikovsky, *Even Granny was Young Once* or M. Hoffman and J. Burroughes, *My Grandma Has Black Hair*; challenge stereotypes about grandparents in the past with stories of brave and active deeds.

11 **Heat and light** – why we need heat and light; types of heating and lighting, including for cooking; interview others about heating and lighting in the past; collect and sequence artefacts; analyse pictures; stories of those who brought about changes, e.g. Edison; life in

different buildings in the past with different forms of heating and lighting; why heating and lighting have improved; imagine life without modern heating and lighting – how would pupils feel?

12 **Games and toys** – favourite toys today and those of relatives; sequence toys, either in pictures or brought from home; discuss similarities and differences as well as the main features of toys; draw and label; why toys have changed, e.g. technological changes such as electricity, plastic, electronics; sort toys into different categories chosen by pupils or teachers; write stories about toys; playground games and nursery rhymes now and in the past – the meaning of rhymes; stories associated with rhymes; separating fact from fiction; toys and games from the distant past, e.g. Ancient Egypt, Vikings.

13 **Food, drink and cooking** – favourite foods and drinks; surveys; how food is obtained, e.g. bought frozen, cooked; discuss with relatives foods and drinks of the past; how they were made and bought; cooking and kitchens – discuss and sequence kitchen and cooking artefacts; stories about food, drinks and eating in the past, from different countries and cultures as well Britain, e.g. rationing in war, medieval food, Tudor feasts, Ancient Egypt, Indians, Romans; pictures of kitchens and dining rooms in the past; written descriptions of feasts; set up home corner as a kitchen from the past; visit museum or site to look at kitchens and dining rooms; study adverts and menus; healthy and unhealthy foods and eating habits now and in the past.

14 **Movement** – how people move and why; how movement changes with age; how people move now; find out, including by interviewing parents and grandparents, how people moved around in the past; list changes; talk about why things have changed; imagine people moving to a particular place now and then; look at pictures showing movement at different times – land, sea and air; sequence and discuss similarities and differences; stories of people who travelled in the past, e.g. Romans, Columbus, Tudor voyager, early aviator or railway pioneer; moving house and why, look at censuses for birthplaces of people and how far they moved; stories of people moving in the past, e.g. to escape famine in Ireland or to come to new lands, e.g. Vikings; early movement to America; travels across America, possibly using stories such as Waddell and Dupasquier, *Going West*.

15 **Time** – how we tell the time now; how we measured time in the past, e.g. sundials, candle clocks, water clocks, grandfather clocks, calendars, diaries; time words; things that happened to pupils at different times, e.g. draw pictures of what happened to them last month and last year; time tunnels for stories at different times in the past, e.g. B. Ball, *Stone Age Magic* or S. Isherwood, *Tim's Knight*; investigate a particular time period and make a timeline; what people wore, ate, lived in and did in the period of their investigation; time capsules; how we find out about times in the past, e.g. archaeology, museums, letters, diaries; stories about evidence from the past, e.g. D. Edwards, *The Baby Angel* (evidence from garden rubbish), Jill Paton Walsh, *Lost and Found* (four stories of lost objects) and M. Dickinson, *Smudge* (a small boy looking for a painting to live in).

16 **Clothes** – types of clothing today, functions, fashions; study pictures of the past; make observations and deductions about clothes and fashion; categorise, e.g. by age, material, function; link fashions to timelines; investigate children's fashions from paintings, photographs and film; interview parents and grandparents about clothes; clothes for different

purposes and different cultures and religions, e.g. work, holidays, leisure, armour for war; stories of people associated with particular clothes; imaginative work and role play about lifestyles associated with particular styles; visit a museum to look at fashions at particular times.

17 **Leisure and holidays** (see the example on page 88).

18 **Places** – different types of place that pupils know; places they have visited recently; which places are old and which new; how they know; what their favourites are and why; places and their different functions; find out about the way certain places have changed, e.g. through pictures and photographs, talking to grandparents, trails and visits; list similarities and differences; find out about and imagine lifestyles associated with places in the past; visit a particular place and investigate functions, lifestyles, changes in detail, e.g. a railway station, a castle; distinguish real events from fiction associated with such places, e.g. dragons, Sleeping Beauty.

Detailed examples of **Myself and my family** and **Leisure and holidays** are provided on pages 86-90

During Key Stage 1 we would like pupils to know and to have frequent opportunities to use the following terms:

TERMS AND CONCEPTS

'What specific terms and concepts should we try to get over to pupils and reinforce through regular use?'

■ morning, afternoon, night, yesterday, today, tomorrow;

■ seconds, minutes, hours, o'clock;

■ days of the week, months, seasons;

■ before, after, then, now, first, last, beginning, middle, end, long ago, last year, this year, next year, past, in the past, once upon a time;

■ event;

■ decade, century, generation;

■ memories, remember.

SOURCES WE THINK PUPILS ARE CAPABLE OF AND INTERESTED IN USING

'What types of source might we want to use with pupils of this age?'

1 **Adults** talking about the past – we think this is very important for almost any topic. We would hope that pupils would be well prepared and would devise questions to ask. Sometimes this would be done in school where we could use familiar people where possible, such as parents, grandparents or cleaners, but also people who are involved in history such as museum people. Sometimes we would hope that children would 'interview' their parents at home.

2 **Advertisements,** including those that illustrate a historical theme (pupils can relate to these and possibly check images). They can also look at advertisements from the past, e.g. from old newspapers and directories, and compare products and advertising with today. This would be ideal for topics like shops and shopping. Posters are very useful and interest young pupils.

3 **Archaeology** we can reconstruct in the classroom, e.g. sand-trays to illustrate stratigraphy. Science can introduce some experiments on decay and preservation. We might also use information technology. Time capsules can give some idea about burial and later interpretation.

4 **Artefacts,** including time-boxes with feelie bags. Home corners and play areas can make use of historical artefacts related to particular historical events and situations, such as old kitchens, an old school or a room during the Blitz.

5 **Books of all kinds** – we would want pupils to use some topic books and encourage them to make more and more use of our infant library. We would want them to look at fiction. Although they would need to be used with care, we could even find uses for comics so that pupils can see how historical characters are depicted. They can then check them against other depictions.

6 **Buildings** – individual buildings, both inside and outside, as well as variety in an area: considering not just homes but also buildings such as shops, churches, schools, cinemas, theatres, factories, stations. We should not get too bogged down with the design of buildings, although this is an excellent way to foster a grasp of change; we should not forget the people who lived in them. One approach we might encourage is to get pupils to think about a story an old house might tell if it could talk. We might stray beyond buildings to cover airfields, parks, fields, etc.

7 **Census** – pupils can often cope with the names and the information is fairly straightforward and familiar. Although we need to be careful about the amount of material and the handwriting, the census can be used on topics such as families, travel, movement, places, homes. We also see huge potential for developing IT and mathematical skills.

8 **Children's games and toys** – since so many of our topics are likely to put an emphasis on children, we would want to make use of games and toys from the past.

9 **Coins and stamps** – apart from being useful for topics such as shops and shopping, pupils can carry out deductions and observations.

10 **Costumes** – obviously good for topics on clothes and families. The ideal is to have some in school, but the next best thing is pictures or visits to a museum. Activities should extend beyond dressing up.

11 **Doll's house** – we can change the layout to show evidence of different lifestyles or furniture.

12 **Gravestones, memorials, inscriptions and statues** – we can see plenty of uses for these and they do not involve the pupils in too much travel. Pupils can learn about other families, events, designs, childhood and beliefs. We might also investigate brass rubbings, which are very good for topics such as clothes.

13 **Information technology** – some simple databases, e.g. names, houses, jobs. We also need to look hard at concept keyboard overlays so that pupils can investigate historical and archaeological diagrams.

14 **Living History** – this is an under-used source. We can organise special days when the pupils have practical experiences of people, situations, periods and events. Aim to do this once every year so pupils can experience 'being' Victorian scholars or makers of Stone Age tools and pottery.

15 **Maps and plans** – we would want to limit these but we can look at some historical plans, e.g. the old and new school and the local area, and possibly some plans using concept keyboard overlays.

16 **Museums** – we don't want to overdo a good thing, but there are obvious uses and they are keen to help our younger pupils. A couple of points, though: any visit should be well planned to link in with what we are covering in school; its focus should always be limited to a few objects, and we also want pupils to think about the way things are laid out and labelled. This will help their understanding of depictions,

interpretations and representations. We also want to make frequent use of class and school museums. We want pupils to bring objects from home. Try to encourage them to talk about the objects, sequence them, consider their uses, write about them and categorise them. They might put old objects and their modern equivalents together, e.g. candle and light-bulb. We would like pupils to feel comfortable in museums so that they will want to visit them with their parents.

17 **Music** – songs as well as tunes from different ages ideal for discussing with adults. Also include rhymes and ditties.

18 **Pictures, drawings, photographs, short extracts of film** (including some black and white) – we should choose sources which allow pupils to detect obvious similarities and differences, such as street scenes at different times. We must not forget postcards as a way of developing these skills (some of which are now available as collections in books). Be a little careful with group pictures – a good starting point can be school and family groups.

19 **Place names** – useful for topics such as the local area. We can use names of towns and villages, fields, streets and houses. Why not link these with stories of the people who gave the names?

20 **Pupils themselves** – they can be a historical source with memories and experiences. They can be an ideal way to illustrate that there can be different ways of looking at the same event. Older pupils can be interviewed by younger pupils about their memories and experiences.

21 **Story** – We are keen to use a wide variety of stories including fiction, myths and legends and eyewitness accounts, especially where it helps pupils develop a sense of sequence and an understanding of evidence and period. Stories can be both read and told. They should not be too complex – a couple of main characters with drama, action and some suspense, ideally demonstrating some strong themes such as bravery and cowardice.

22 **Television and radio** – We need to be selective. There are some obvious gems, e.g. *Watch*, but the activities need to be well planned and the use limited to sensibly sized extracts. However, television and radio can enhance almost any topic and provide variety.

23 **Theme parks** to link into topics, e.g. explorers, schools.

24 **Timelines of various kinds** – we would hope that these would include horizontal timelines noting personal, family and other events. However, we will have a large wall timeline in each classroom. There can also be circular timecharts showing events in a day, seasons, years, etc. Other variations might include a washing line with clothes pegs; folding, zig-zag timelines; time snakes; pictorial timecharts. There should be a gradual move towards some kind of scale, but this may not be appropriate with the youngest pupils.

25 **Written sources with limited writing** – familiar and personal sources would be ideal. These can include tickets, brief letters, a diary entry, ration books, birth certificates, school log books.

KEY IDEAS

'Are there any key ideas we would want to get over to pupils and reinforce during the key stage?'

We should like our Key Stage 1 pupils to understand with increasing sophistication the following 'historical ideas':

■ a world existed before both they and those around them were born;

■ there are different ways of describing the past, using words such as days of the week, yesterday, today, long ago, new, old;

■ the past was different to the present but there are similarities;

■ people in the past had feelings, ideas and attitudes;

■ people make things happen, so some happenings are planned; things do not just happen;

■ people are affected by events;

■ we can tell different stories about the same event;

■ there are different ways of showing what happened in the past, e.g. stories, pictures;

■ we can disagree about what happened in the past and it does not necessarily mean that one of us is wrong;

■ people from the past left relics of their lives but they did not leave everything;

■ often there are not enough clues to tell us the full story about the past.

Individual topics

The two examples which follow offer suggestions only on the history aspects of the two topics. Most Key Stage 1 teachers would clearly want to incorporate these themes within a general topic.

MYSELF AND MY FAMILY

1 **Who am I?** What is my name? Charts of class names. What do I look like? Drawings and labels. What feelings and emotions do I have? Make a list and draw expressions such as happiness and sadness on a face. Do others in the class interpret the expressions as you mean them to? Get them to think about senses. There may be opportunities for telling stories about people in the past who were able to do remarkable things without having these senses, e.g. Beethoven, Helen Keller, Blind Jack of Knaresborough.

2 **What is a family?** How many brothers and sisters do you have? With sensitivity, discuss this and also parents and grandparents – put them in order of age. What are the signs that someone is older? Draw pictures of people at different ages. Show a family picture. Get pupils to identify the oldest and youngest. The concept of family could be reinforced by using stories such as the *My Family* series. There may also be opportunities to illustrate different viewpoints by using stories such as Judy Blume's *The Pain and the Great One*, where the events are seen from the viewpoints of different family members.

3 **What is my history?** Explain that they have not always been the same age. It is important for them to understand that time moves on and people move along with it. This needs constant reinforcement. Strategies might include making diaries about events over a week, producing their own daily timeline, having movable arrows noting yesterday, today and tomorrow so that they are reminded that they are constantly changing. What is their earliest memory? Draw it. Get the whole class to draw an event which they all witnessed yesterday, such as the weather. Discuss different depictions.

Pupils could think of four or five events in their lives, such as their birth or that of a brother or sister, starting school, breaking an arm, memorable holidays, etc. Indicate to pupils that different people have different experiences and 'important' events in their lives. Pupils could produce a brief personal timeline. They can bring in some photographs of themselves at different ages and put these in order on a personal timeline. The frequent use of time words and the notion of events happening at a particular point in time needs constant coverage by drawing events from different times in their lives such as last week, last month, last year.

Pupils could also be encouraged to ask parents what they were like as babies and what type of things they themselves can do now which they could not do as babies. The sequencing exercise could then be tried out with someone older, e.g. a teacher (if brave enough) or parents. There would be some opportunity to discuss incidental matters such as changes in fashion, hairstyle, background. One issue that may need to be addressed is that young pupils find it difficult to distinguish the age of a person in the photograph from the age of the photograph itself; they need to understand that the younger the person is in the picture, the older the photograph. It is also important to get over the message that black and white photographs are not necessarily the oldest.

4 **Was my 'personal history' the same as older people's?** It is important for pupils to understand that older people were once young. There are stories that can be used to help get this message across, e.g. E. Janikovsky, *Even Granny Was Young Once* and M. Williams, *When I Was Little*. Either at home or in school, an elderly person such as a grandparent can be 'interviewed'. Questions need to be prepared carefully in advance and the interviewee properly briefed. The focus should be limited. Popular themes include life at home, food, school, leisure including toys, games and holidays, fashions, music, and things that made them happy and sad such as war or holidays. If everyone in the class hears the same account, there may be opportunities for older pupils to note differences in the versions.

Pupils then need to follow up the information. Get them to consider how we know about things that have happened. Areas which may be followed up are memories, museums, people talking about things, photographs, pictures, objects, letters, old buildings. Show some of these to the pupils. This can generate discussion. Pupils could also be asked to categorise sources, distinguishing paintings from photographs and realistic pictures of the past from depictions, say, in comics.

Pupils could be asked to discuss and sequence a few objects from the past. For instance, they could describe and draw them, note six things about an object and try to work out what it was used for. They might be asked to categorise the objects, e.g. to say which room in a house they belonged in. There may be opportunities to return to the theme of senses and link sources to the various senses, e.g. touch (artefacts), hearing (oral history and songs) and sight (pictures, buildings), and to get pupils to think about how they are using their senses to work out something from one of these sources.

5 **Are there other ways we can find out about people in the past?** Although Key Stage 1 will inevitably have a strong focus on visual material and artefacts, it is as well if pupils realise that people wrote things down in the past, and that some of this writing is still available to us today. Although it will have to be used with great care, the census

offers some opportunity for simple counting and interpretation. Explain clearly to pupils that the census was a list made of everyone living in houses a long time ago. Pupils could each be given two or three houses from the local census (say 1871 or 1881) to focus on. They could obtain information about the number of children living in each house and their ages, the names people had and jobs they did, such as servants. This could lead to some imaginative work, such as writing and possibly a role play about life in a particular household. They could do name surveys and compare names people had then and now.

6 **What about other families?** Discuss the diversity of family experiences. There may be opportunities to look at these in times of crisis, e.g. through stories such as the Aahlbergs', *Peepo* and J. Talbot, *The Raries* (both about World War II). However, cultural diversity should also be covered. Use the experiences of Asian and African children and tell stories of families in the past. Good story lines can emerge about families in Ancient Egypt or the Indus Valley, focusing particularly on the role of children. Contrasting experiences might also involve stories about the children of a king or queen (e.g. the childhood of Elizabeth I) and those growing up in poor family at the time of the Industrial Revolution (introducing the issue of child labour – *The Water Babies*, etc.). There is enough visual evidence to accompany these examples. There may even be opportunities for pupils to investigate in class or library topic books. Teachers should use every opportunity to ask questions about how we know about these events which happened a long time ago. One of the key ideas referred to on page 86 relates to our reliance on relics and remains from the past for information.

7 **The conclusion.** The topic could conclude with a display of objects from times in the past and pictures and drawings of life in our grandparents' time, and the completion of a class timeline showing the important events and personalities covered. There may even be an opportunity for a role play about an event pupils have covered or about a particular child's experience in the past. Another possibility is the preparation of a time capsule. Some pupils might like to think about what they would put in a time capsule today which would allow people a long time ahead to understand them. Another group of pupils might like to do it for their grandparents' time.

LEISURE AND HOLIDAYS   1 **Starting point.** Show a holiday picture with children at the seaside. Discuss favourite types of holiday. Where have pupils been to on holiday? What did they enjoy when they were there? Is there anything they did not enjoy? How did they travel there? Use maps showing location. Carry out a simple analysis, e.g. how many went to the seaside? How many went by car? What did they take with them on holiday? Sensitivity will need to be used with those who rarely if ever go on holiday. Care will also need to be taken to ensure that holidays are interpreted as 'using holiday time' and that there is no special kudos to travelling large distances and going to exotic places. Show as much interest and spend as much time talking to pupils who did nothing more than play football on the common or visit Gran in the next street. One could also sequence holiday times on a timeline. Pupils could then be asked why most people go on holiday in the summer months.

2 **Did our parents and grandparents go on holiday?** This can be established by 'interviewing' them. The points worth investigating include where they went, how they got there, what was the furthest they ever travelled, what they did when they got there and any difficulties. Pupils could then be asked to make a list of differences in the types of

holiday, and also a list of similarities. Any ideas about why things are different today would be worth exploring. There may also be opportunities to use stories associated both with grandparents and holidays such as I. Gantschev, *The Train to Grandma's*.

Pupils could hear a story about a typical holiday, say, in the 1950s. They could be asked to retell it using a series of cards which they have to sequence. They could also add captions to the cards. Another activity might involve the removal of a couple of cards. Pupils would then have to work out which cards had been removed. Yet another alternative is to leave the story incomplete and get pupils to work out an ending. However, this would be better done when they have a better grasp of life at that time – perhaps nearer the end of the topic.

Pupils could look at some historical sources about holidays; there is no shortage of pictures and photographs of seaside and beauty spot scenes in different decades. They could comment on pictures showing different leisure pursuits, e.g. cycling holidays, rich people cruising on a great ocean liner, bank holiday railway scenes, bathing huts, people at great sporting events, fairgrounds and circuses, camping holidays. A series of scenes, both from today and from different periods in the past, could be jumbled up in a pack. Pupils could be asked to categorise the scenes into piles, for example, travel scenes, seaside scenes, pier scenes, sports, etc., as well as to sequence them. They should be asked why they have placed the sources in a particular order.

There may be opportunities to focus in depth on one particular aspect, such as clothes on holiday. Pupils could consider what types of clothes they take on holiday. Then, by looking at pictures of different ages, they could note and sequence changing fashions, by making drawings and placing them on a timeline. There may also be opportunities for them to compare a holiday scene at two different dates: pupils could circle or list differences. Ask pupils which of the two scenes they would like to have been part of and why.

There might also be opportunities to focus in some detail on a particular type of source such as pictures and photographs. They could explore how photographs are taken and look at cameras of different ages (perhaps from a museum) or at least pictures of these cameras. They could also be encouraged to develop their skills of distinguishing pictures from photographs, as well as realistic from unrealistic holiday scenes, e.g. Firth's Victorian railway scene from pictures of animals in clothes on holiday. There could be a mixture of obvious and less obvious pictures including cartoons and postcards. Pupils should be asked to give reasons for their observations and deductions. Other questions could relate to the importance of specific people and events in pictures and photographs.

3 **How were people encouraged to go on holiday?** This helps pupils to understand that documents can sometimes be used as a means to influence. There are various examples which can be used, from past and present, such as travel brochures and posters (the early railway and resort posters, such as 'Skegness is So Bracing', are fairly accessible in facsimile form). Pupils could be asked about their appeal and could then design their own to try to influence people to go to a particular place they know.

4 **Who helps us to have a good holiday?** Pupils could be asked to think about people who work in the holiday business, e.g. travel agents, train and coach drivers, sailors and pilots, hoteliers, fairground owners, those

who work at the seaside. It might be possible to interview someone in the holiday business and ask them how the job has changed over the years. Pupils could follow this up by looking at pictures such as railway scenes and investigating how these have changed. There may be opportunities for role playing a scene from the viewpoint of someone involved in the holiday business. The home corner may also include a holiday scene such as a hotel reception or a booking office.

5 **The mysterious holiday-maker.** This is a well-tried and tested approach designed to get pupils thinking about evidence. The scene can be set for them. For example, they are on a train just reaching their holiday destination when they notice that somebody has left a suitcase behind. They wonder who it belongs to. They open it and find all kinds of belongings such as clothes, tickets, brochures, artefacts. Their task is to find out something about the holiday-maker, e.g. age, sex, size, interests, from the objects inside. To give a historical dimension, some historical artefacts might be placed in the case to stimulate some discussion. Pupils should be encouraged to note 'what they can definitely tell', 'what they can probably deduce' and 'further questions they would like to ask'.

6 **The conclusion.** Various possibilities exist, such as a frieze and timeline for the wall or a class book on holidays in the past. There could be some creative writing demonstrating pupils' understanding of the excitement and nature of a holiday in the past. The classroom museum should be added to with displays of holiday brochures, photographs, souvenirs and other artefacts. There may be scope for making a presentation to an audience, e.g. Year 2 pupils could explain the exhibits to reception pupils.

4.2 Key Stage 2 history

General considerations

Although most of this section concentrates on individual study units, some introduction is probably called for to discuss the particularly difficult problem of differentiation. Since study units in Key Stage 2 can be taught in any order and may, indeed, be taught to different aged pupils in the same class or school, it is important to consider the validity of content and activities for individual pupils. There will be many activities which are appropriate across the key stage, as the same ideas and skills often need reinforcing and applying across different contexts. However, it would be wrong to assume that this is always the case.

The section on Key Stage 1 considered the general problems and opportunities presented to pupils. Examples 4.2 and 4.3 here summarise the general guidance provided by the coordinator in one school. Although research has indicated the dangers of trying to divide up competencies according to ages, Example 4.2 was based on close scrutiny of research evidence and classroom observation. This is followed in Example 4.3 by a more general list of key skills and ideas which need to be established and developed during the key stage. The coordinator encouraged teachers to use these ideas and skills when covering particular study units.

EXAMPLE 4.2: ACTIVITIES WE MIGHT TRY OUT WITH OUR CLASSES

Year 3
- spotting broad differences in time such as then/now and before/after;

- spotting broad differences in place such as here/there and them/us;

- observing quite small details in sources such as pictures and artefacts;

- family trees;

- grasping the essentials of a whole story including the most significant events and personalities;

- understanding why somebody may have wanted to do something;

- understanding what may have happened as a result of an event or action;

- sequencing five or six events or artefacts;

- drawing some conclusions about sources such as artefacts;

- distinguishing differences in sources, e.g. between pictures and photographs;

- gathering information from more than one source;

- working in groups;

- researching in the library.

N.B. When sequencing, pupils may find the use of Roman numerals difficult. They will also find change difficult to understand, seeing it more as a series of direct actions and the substitution of one thing for another.

Year 4
- detecting continuity;

- timelines and sequencing of six or seven objects or events;

- some grasp of more complex time terms, e.g. ancient, modern, BC;

- linking causes and effects;

- offering a reasonable explanation for some events;

- asking a variety of questions;

- simple deductions and inferences;

- arranging and expressing information in short paragraphs;

- some comparisons across events and periods;

- simple evaluation of some evidence;

■ reading and comprehending a range of historical sources;

■ participating in organised group work;

■ showing some independence and initiative.

N.B. Pupils may have difficulty detecting patterns and relationships between historical situations and events. Their limited numeracy skills may also cause problems with dates.

Year 5

■ retelling a story from the viewpoint of somebody involved;

■ coping with up to 1000 years in time;

■ using period labels;

■ producing and making use of multi-dimensional timelines;

■ using timescales when referring to changes;

■ using new time words, e.g. contemporary;

■ matching dates to people and events;

■ grasping different types of change and how the change has taken place;

■ using the language of probability when offering reasons and results;

■ explaining a strange attitude or decision somebody has made;

■ showing some grasp of the thoughts and feelings of others, including sympathy;

■ making inferences about the viewpoints of others;

■ showing a grasp of causation as well as motivation and noting a variety of causes and effects;

■ offering some reasons for different versions of events;

■ being able to use a degree of specificity with regard to labels, e.g. a German candle holder; a Scottish infantryman;

■ producing reasonable accounts – up to four paragraphs;

■ organising and planning displays;

■ showing independence and initiative in group activities.

N.B. Pupils may still have difficulties with four-digit dates.

Year 6

■ grasping that society is more than a series of unrelated individuals;

■ detecting change and continuity and commenting on these, e.g. rates of change, types of change, whether progress has been made;

■ sound time sense using dates, periods, eras, BC and AD;

■ sequencing around ten features on timelines;

■ recognising and applying different causes and results to investigations;

■ analysing the motives of others including groups;

■ understanding and using a good range of original documents;

■ studying several aspects of history simultaneously;

■ planning and carrying out independent investigations;

■ understanding the beliefs of others including some that are conflicting;

■ thinking of ways of checking the accuracy of depictions and interpretations;

■ linking events and actions;

■ extended communication including use of sub-headings, maps and diagrams;

■ good group work such as group investigations and reports.

N.B. There may still be confusion over overlapping terms, e.g. Tudors and 16th century. Pupils may also be confused if everything is depicted as too tentative, uncertain and provisional.

The above was never intended to be all embracing, or even for elements to follow on from one year to the next. It was simply intended to be a reminder to teachers of some of the things they may consider using with 'average' pupils in particular years.

At the same time as making the list in Example 4.2, the coordinator was keen for teachers to plan their history teaching against a checklist of key ideas and skills. These were not intended to relate to particular classes or pupils. Instead, they were regarded as essential and in need of frequent reinforcement. Teachers were told that they were unlikely to over-provide, unless coverage reduced the time available to develop pupils' other skills and ideas.

EXAMPLE 4.3: KEY SKILLS AND IDEAS TO TEACH AND REINFORCE

Skills and competencies
■ answer historical questions and solve historical problems;

■ ask questions and suggest their own investigations;

■ carry out investigations using reference, selection, organisational and synthesis skills;

■ suggest ideas and hypotheses to answer historical questions;

■ detect patterns, links and connections between events, periods and perspectives;

■ use historical terms and language;

■ argue about what is important with regard to motives, causes, events, results, etc.;

■ explain historical events and situations;

■ piece together evidence to explain a particular event or scene;

■ present a logical argument;

■ present history in appropriate formats such as written and oral work, wall displays, role plays, family trees, group reports;

■ frequently use a range of time words and ideas including period labels, dates, sequencing and different forms of timelines;

■ be accurate;

■ explore alternatives and choices including those available to people at the time of an historical event;

■ put historical causes, effects or events in order of importance;

■ recognise and discuss conflicting views;

■ understand many of the techniques and procedures used by the historian;

■ know about and understand different types of source and the problems and benefits involved in using them, e.g. authenticity, distortion;

■ translate historical sources from one medium to another;

■ recall historical information and the way that history is produced;

■ make inferences and deductions;

■ summarise the main features and issues including conclusions and generalisations;

■ work in different social situations, e.g. individually, in pairs, in groups and in whole–class situations.

Ideas
■ The past is connected to the present.

■ Some things have changed whereas others have remained largely the same over time. Where change has occurred, it has at times happened rapidly and at others more slowly.

■ Not all changes have been good for everyone. Change can lead to progress for some but regression for others.

■ Things usually happen for reasons.

■ As today, things in the past did not always go according to plan.

■ People in the past had feelings, beliefs and attitudes. They are not necessarily the same viewpoints and feelings as we have today.

■ When faced with decisions, people often had more than one choice.

■ Not everyone who lived in the past shared the same views and feelings.

■ There are different types of cause and consequence, e.g. social, religious and political, short-term and long-term, and some are more important than others. A particular type of cause does not always produce that type of result, e.g. an economic cause does not necessarily just produce an economic result.

■ There can be different versions of the same event, or different descriptions of the same person and it does not necessarily mean that some of them are wrong. People can disagree for valid reasons.

■ Sometimes history is inaccurate and does not present a fair view of somebody or something in the past.

■ There are many ways we can put together the events of the past, e.g. story, written account, film, picture.

■ We can all create history. Although we may all follow the same rules we might not all end up with the same result. History is not something out there waiting to be caught in a net. We make it like a sculpture out of materials. In the case of history, the materials are the remains from the past.

■ The remains from the past come in many different forms, e.g. written, oral, tangible. They are not evenly spread out. For some periods and events they are too sparse, but for others they are too abundant. There is just not enough time to investigate and cover everything. What you select obviously affects the version.

■ The quality and quantity of the evidence from the past and the care taken to investigate it affect the quality of the history. Some history is more reliable than other history.

■ It is not just a matter of finding the sources. There can be problems in using them. They are not always accurate or reliable. People were not always honest or fair when they produced the source. We should try to work out whether a source is reliable and what sort of questions it can be used to answer.

■ Not everything from the past is uncertain. Some historical information is fairly 'safe' and not really disputed.

■ With care, we can get a great deal of information from many sources.

The study units

The rest of this book provides possible approaches to each of the Key Stage 2 study units. The following study units are included:

1 Romans, Anglo-Saxons and Vikings in Britain – an overview with separate plans for each of the three groups of settlers; page 97

2 Life in Tudor Times; page 118

3a Victorian Britain; page 128

3b Britain since 1930; page 138

4 Ancient Greece; page 145

5 Local History: The Local Railway; page 155

6 Non-European Civilisation: Ancient Egypt; page 159

Each unit adopts the same format, using the planning matrix on page 33. More complete details about the planning matrix can be found on those pages 32–36. In summary, the columns are:

Column 1 Main Investigations, in the form of key questions.

Column 2 Key Content areas.

Column 3 Pupil Experiences, suggesting a range of activities and resources. The suggestions are likely to exceed the time available in most primary schools, but schools may like to select from within the list.

Column 4 Approaches to differentiation, using the following code:
1 undifferentiated work – designed for all pupils;
2 differentiation by group – separate tasks for different groups;
3 differentiation by outcome – common tasks but different outputs;
4 differentiation by task;
5 differentiated source material;
6 differentiated resources;
7 differentiation by teacher input;
8 differentiation by time.

Column 5 Key Elements.

Column 6 Assessment Opportunities, using the following code:
A everyday written work;
B special tasks with specific objectives;
C formal tasks and tests;
D observing pupils in action;
E questioning pupils using interviews or discussions;
F self or peer-group evaluation.

Column 7 Links to other subjects and cross-curricular themes and dimensions.

A note about resources

Most of the resources mentioned in Column 3 are easily available, many of them from major educational publishers. We have not given bibliographic details in such cases as the latest publishers' catalogues will usually be available in schools.

However, as some recommended resources are likely to be more difficult to find a list of addresses is provided at pages 166–67.

ROMANS, ANGLO-SAXONS AND VIKINGS IN BRITAIN

Main investigations	Key content	Pupil experiences	Differentiation	Key Elements	Assessment opportunities	Links
OVERVIEW						
1 Who were these people and where did they come from?	Main groups of people	Discuss what an invasion is. Difference between 'conquest' and 'settlement'.	1	5b	D, E	
	Where they came from	Draw and talk about maps showing where they came from and where they settled. Use different colours and overlays. Introduce idea of conflict and cooperation. Work on distances.	3	2a, 2b, 2c, 5a, 5c	A	Geography Citizenship Maths
	When did they arrive? Chronology	Timelines. Tasks especially on BC and AD. Stress sporadic nature of settlement and intermingling. Settlement included black peoples.	3, 6, 7	1a, 1b, 2c	B, E	Equal opportunities
	Nature of settlement	Pupils work out problems settlers may have faced. Where would they choose? Investigate where they settled in Britain. Pupils think why?	3, 4, 7	2a, 2b, 2c, 4a, 4b, 5a, 5c	A, D, E	
	Wider context	Investigate where else these peoples went, e.g. Roman Empire, Viking America. Map and distance work.	3, 7	4a, 4b, 5a, 5c	A, D	Geography Maths
	Local settlement	Fit any local information onto timelines. Use any knowledge and materials pupils have.	1, 2, 7	1a, 2c, 5a, 5c	A, D, E	
2 Why should they want to come?	Britain on the eve of the Roman invasion	Imaginative work using pictures or source material. Pupils piece together evidence to investigate whether it was backward.	3, 5, 7	2a, 2b, 3a	B	
	Celtic life	Structured investigation and questions on Celtic life, e.g. forestry, food, farming, clothes, role of women. Use posters, published resources.	3, 4, 6, 7, 8	2a, 2b, 4a, 4c, 5a, 5b, 5c	A, D, E	Geography Economic & industrial understanding

Main investigations	Key content	Pupil experiences	Differentiation	Key Elements	Assessment opportunities	Links
2 contd	The advantages and disadvantages of invasion	Pupils consider why people should want to come. Who would benefit and who lose out? Creative writing.	3, 7	2b, 5c	D, E	English – writing
	Conflict and cooperation	What is friendship? Why do people fall out? Use personal examples to show benefits of cooperation. Pupils list the kind of things they can do on their own and when they need to use others.	1, 7	2a, 5b, 5c	A, D, E	Citizenship
	Reasons for Roman, Saxon and Viking invasions	Investigate causes listed in books including sources. Compare reasons given in different books and for different peoples.	3, 5, 6, 7, 8	2a, 2b, 2c, 4a, 4b, 5a, 5b, 5c	B, D, E	IT English
3 What did they do when they reached Britain?	What did they use and what did they destroy?	Pupils work out what they might use and what they would do with the people. Would they have slaves? Investigate or inform what happened.	3, 6, 7	2a, 2b, 4a, 4b	A, D, E	Citizenship English
	Decisions to take and problems to solve	Either problems posed by teacher or IT simulations available (for Romans, Anglo–Saxons and Vikings).	2, 3, 4, 7, 8	2a, 2b, 4a, 4b, 5a, 5b, 5c	B, D, E	IT
	The local scene	Link what happened locally using evidence.	1	2a	A	
	Areas of control	Investigate areas of control and consider reasons why some, e.g. south-west and Scotland, were difficult to control. Map work.	3, 7, 8	2a, 2b, 2c, 4a, 4b, 5a, 5c	B, D, E	Geography
		Reinforcement work on timelines.	3	1a, 2c, 5a	B	Maths
	Resistance and rebellion	Imaginative work – how would they have resisted? Investigation or information about main rebellions and resistance, e.g. Boudicca. Can use stories, e.g. Sally Harris, *Son of Rebellion* published by Anglia Young Books.	3, 6, 7	2a, 2b, 4a, 4b, 5a, 5b, 5c	A, D	English

Key question	Focus	Teaching activities				Cross-curricular links
4 What has each group left behind that we have today?	Place-names and other names Landmarks in town and country	Work on locating them, e.g. in locality using maps, reference books. Research meaning of days, months, festivals. Find other words in dictionaries of Romans, Saxons, Vikings. Slides, pictures, posters and information in books, e.g. Hadrian's Wall, Offa's Dyke, Jorvik, Roman roads, Saxon churches. Discuss survivals; produce pageant. Compare survivals. Talk about purposes of landmarks. Why do we preserve them? Place on class or pupil timeline.	3, 5, 6, 7, 8	4a, 4b, 5a, 5b	A, B, D	Geography English Environmental education
				1a, 2a, 2b, 2c, 4a, 4b, 5a, 5b, 5c	A, D, E	
	Gaps in evidence	Need to get over idea that we do not know everything about peoples. Pupils consider problems if a society did not write much. Link to these peoples.	1	3a		
			3, 7	4a, 4b	A, E	
	Archaeology	How do we know? Introduce or reinforce basic features of archaeology, e.g. examine some artefacts from sand tray; class and record; use grids; wash and record or use general or specific IT simulation, e.g. *Unearthing the Past* by CUP; *Expedition to Saqqara* published by Ginn; English Heritage video *Archaeological Detectives* - Investigating a site or archaeology detective poster. Comments on some artefacts and infer about use and user, e.g. coins, boneware, leatherware, metalwork. Can be pictures from book.	3, 5, 7, 8	2a, 2c, 4a, 4b, 5c	B, D, E	Science IT Technology
			2, 3, 5, 7, 8			
5 Did Romans, Anglo-Saxons and Vikings live similar lives?	Brief comparisons of aspects of life, e.g. homes, lifestyle, technology, transport, role of women, children	Give particular members of class a theme to investigate: a) distinctive features; b) what changed; c) what stayed the same. Encourage pictorial representations on timelines. Whole-class feedback. Give higher attainers more complex material and aspects.	2, 4, 5, 6, 7	1a, 2a, 2b, 2c, 4a, 4b, 5a, 5b, 5c	A, D, E	Science Equal opportunities

Main investigations	Key content	Pupil experiences	Differentiation	Key Elements	Assessment opportunities	Links
5 contd		Sequence and discuss objects and place on timeline or sort into peoples. Who might have used them and why, e.g. jewellery, toys, transport and farming implements. N.B. Avoid the myth of the huge gulf between technologically superior Romans and others. Include sources stressing art and culture of Saxons and Vikings or the more active role of Saxon women, e.g. in landholding, church and education.	3, 4, 5, 7	1a, 1b, 2a, 2b, 2c	B, D, E	Technology Maths Equal opportunities

ROMANS

1 What sort of country did the Romans come to?	Landscape People The built environment	Use books and/or sources including pictures to show Romans came to a rural, heavily forested land with few towns, well-established trade, hill forts, farms and villages with separate, often conflicting groups.	3, 4, 5, 6, 7	1a, 2a, 2c, 4a, 4b, 5a, 5b, 5c	A, D, E	Geography Citizenship English
	Economy	Draw picture based on evidence.				
		See if depictions seem accurate.		3a	B	
	The local scene	Compare main differences now and then – what would a time traveller most notice?		1a, 2a, 2c		
		What evidence exists for the Romans in the locality? Story or brief investigation.	2, 8	4a, 4b, 5a, 5c	A, D, E	
2 Why did Romans come to Britain?	Roman Empire – conquest, settlement	Decision-making – why do people invade? Would pupils have chosen to come?	3, 7	2b	A, E	
	– Caesar 55BC and first invasion	Character description. Use published resources and original sources. Would they like to have been led by him? Descriptive or narrative writing or cartoon/ drawings with sequencing and captions. Discuss different depictions.	3, 5, 6, 7	1a, 2a, 2b, 2c, 4a, 4b, 5a, 5b, 5c	A, B, D, E	English – writing
				3a		
	Claudius and AD43 invasion	Consider reasons. Higher attainers might devise hierarchy of important reasons, e.g. military glory, greed, need for more land. Would they prefer to have been led by Claudius or Caesar? Give reasons.	3, 7	2a, 2b	B, E	Geography
			2, 8	2b, 3a	A, E	
	Evidence – archaeological, written	Develop pupils' grasp of archaeology, e.g. IT Arcventure simulation. Examine a local or national Roman site, e.g. Lullingstone, North Leigh (English Heritage), Chedworth (National Trust). Discuss aspects – deductions about	3, 4, 5, 6, 7	2a, 2c, 4a, 4b, 5a, 5b, 5c	A, D, E	Technology Science

Main investigations	Key content	Pupil experiences	Differentiation	Key Elements	Assessment opportunities	Links
2 contd		buildings in towns, villas or artefacts. Reproduction artefacts, e.g. oil lamps, beakers, coins, spoons, spindles, tesserae – uses, users, usefulness.				
		Comments on written sources, e.g. Cicero, inscriptions, place names, Tacitus in published books. Use IT, e.g. *Data 100 Appian Way.* Local examples where possible. Pupils consider what they tell us; inaccuracies. Discuss why writers might exaggerate or not tell the truth.	3, 5, 6, 7	3a, 4a, 4b	B, D, E	English – speaking/listening
		Pupils devise questions on sources. Other pupils try to answer questions posed.	2, 3, 8	4a, 4b, 5a, 5c	D, E	
3 How might the Romans be able to gain control?	Roman armies – size, organisation, weapons, life in the army (colonial), defences including Hadrian's Wall	What makes a successful army? Possible group work.	1, 2	2a, 2b	D, E	
		Investigation using a range of appropriate sources, e.g. IT (SEMERC *Just Pictures; My World)*, published books, on aspects such as organisation, training, where legions came from, infantry and cavalry.	3, 5, 6, 7	2a, 2b, 2c, 4a, 4b, 5a, 5b, 5c	A, B, D, E	IT
		Make and/or discuss effectiveness of weapons in different circumstances, e.g. catapults, javelins, stabbing swords.	2, 3, 7, 8	2a, 2b, 5c	A, D, E	Technology
	The local scene	Selective use of sources, e.g. Sutcliff, *Eagle of the Ninth, Eagle's Egg, Circlet of Oak Trees* published by Hamish Hamilton. Compare accuracy with other sources.	2, 8	3a, 4a	A, E	English – reading
		Use sources including site evidence, pictures and writing to produce descriptive accounts of life on Hadrian's Wall. Look at reconstructed drawings, e.g.	3, 5, 6, 7	2a, 2b, 2c, 4a, 4b, 5a, 5b, 5c	A, D, E	English – writing

Key question	Focus	Teaching activities and resources	Study unit	Key elements	Level	Cross-curricular links
3 contd		Sorrell. Should we destroy farming land to excavate sites and open up to the public?	3	3a	E	Environmental education
		Study pictures and other sources to discuss how well Romans defended places, e.g. town walls, earthwork banks, coastal forts. What does it tell us about Roman technology? Mark main sites on a map.	3, 5, 6, 7	4a, 4b, 5a, 5c	B, E	Technology
		Role play/imaginative work on life of a Roman soldier – clothes, weapons, accommodation, play, education, retirement.	1	2a	A, D, E	Drama English
	Native Britons in battle	'Letters' or 'diary' entries. Share with others in class. Why did Britons often not succeed against Romans? Stress their amateur nature, weapons, lack of supplies.	3, 4, 7	2a, 2b, 2c, 5a, 5b, 5c	B, E	Technology
		Link any local information to wider picture.	3, 6, 7	2a, 2b	A	
4 How would you treat the native Britons?	Cooperation or conflict	Pupils use information to decide whether it was better to be cruel or kind. Discuss how you can get people on your side.	3	2a	A, D, E	
	Use of local people by Romans	Use local case study and/or fiction, e.g. Ruth Marris, *The Cornerstone* published by Heinemann.	3, 7	2a, 2b	B, D, E	
	Rebellions especially Boudicca AD61 – character and problems	Research reasons for Boudicca's rebellion, e.g. property confiscation, expulsions, taxes, flogging and rape. Deductions about the role of women.	2	2a, 2b, 2c, 4a, 4b, 5a, 5c	B, E	Equal opportunities
	Other examples of different treatments – cause and effect	Use and comment on sources, especially contrasting views, e.g. Tacitus, later books.	3, 4, 6, 7	4a, 4b	D, E	
		Imaginative work/role play seeing things from different sides (Boudicca was arrogant, had more troops and was herself cruel).	3, 5, 7	2a, 2b, 2c, 5a, 5b, 5c	A, E	
		Use fiction, e.g. Henry Treece, *The Bronze Sword* published by Hamish Hamilton, Sally Harris, *Son of Rebellion* published by Anglia Young Books. Also BEEP materials.	3, 6, 7 / 2	4a, 4b		English – reading

Main investigations	Key content	Pupil experiences	Differentiation	Key Elements	Assessment opportunities	Links
4 contd		Higher attainers can discuss different images and depictions with possible reasons.	2	3a	B, E	
		Talk about how the Romans should have responded to Boudicca. Discuss pupils' views.	3, 7	2a, 2b, 2c	E	
		Inform about other forms of treatment, e.g. Caratacus.	1		A	
5 How civilised was Roman life?	'Romanisation' – AD70–160. How did Romans gain control over much of the country?	Investigation from books or IT simulation e.g. covering advance to west, northern frontier.	3, 6, 7	2a, 2b, 2c, 4a, 4b, 5a, 5b, 5c	A, B, D, E	
		Cover local developments – mark on timeline.		1a, 2c	A, D	
	Latin language	Latin words. Use dictionary to link to today's language.	3, 6, 7, 8	2a, 2c	A, E	English
	Aspects of Roman life, e.g. towns, the countryside, buildings, home life, women and children, clothes, leisure and sports, trade and industry, rich and poor, transport, religion including Constantine and introduction of Christianity and its development as a state religion	Investigations, e.g. group or individual research on aspects with overviews from class reading, whole class information, source work, pictures and sites and possibly a visit to a museum or site.	3, 4, 5, 6, 7, 8	2a, 2b, 2c, 4a, 4b, 5a, 5b, 5c	A, B, D, E	
		A wide range of published resources is available. IT can also be utilised, e.g. ESM's *Isca* looks at life in a Roman town examining architecture, inhabitants, daily life, religion, leisure and occupations; SEMERC's *My World 2*, *Phases* and *Just Pictures*. There are commercial artefacts available to supplement any local loans, e.g. torcs, combs, figures, beakers, coins, spoons, broaches, spindle whorls, glass bangles, tesserae, or visits to sites.	5			IT Art Citizenship
	Roman technology	Activities might include: – discussing technology and designs: effectiveness. Compare today	2, 5			Technology
	Roman towns	– case studies of towns, with imaginative	3, 4, 5, 6, 7	2a, 2b, 2c, 5c		Technology
				2a, 2b, 2c, 4a,		

Theme	Activities				Cross-curricular links
5 contd	writing or role play on buildings and their uses, e.g. forum, basilicas, markets, theatres, amphitheatres, law courts and baths. Use and comment on reconstructions			A, B, D, E	Economic and industrial understanding Environmental education
	– evidence work, reconstructing sites, fieldwork, using facilities at places such as the ARC (York) or Lawns (Lincoln)	3, 5, 6, 7	4b, 5a, 5b, 5c		
	– comparing buildings and towns today, e.g. similarity and difference	3, 4, 5, 6, 7	3a		
Trade and industry	– making deductions about trades, e.g. painters, mosaicists, potters. Practical activities; role plays	3, 5, 6, 7	4a, 4b, 5a, 5c		Technology
Rich and poor	– examining and describing life in a villa, discussing comfort, health, etc., e.g. hypocausts, piped water, glazing, tessellated floors, bath suites	3, 4, 5, 6, 7	2a, 2b, 2c		Economic and industrial understanding Equal opportunities
	– using artefacts to make deductions about lifestyle, uses. Introduce the idea of mass production, e.g. pottery		4a, 4b, 5a, 5b, 5c		
	– group research and reconstruct/narrate a typical day of different types of people, e.g. a town dweller, farmer, builder, shopkeeper, woman, child, slave. Compare lives with today.	2, 3, 5, 6, 7	2a, 2b, 2c, 4a, 4b, 5a, 5b, 5c		
Sport and art	– contrast evidence about cruelty and 'sophistication', e.g. cruel sports, treatment of some people, such as women and children, versus art such as sculptures, mosaics, jewellery, pottery, furniture, household goods, letters sent by soldiers to children. How can this be explained?	3, 5, 6, 7			Citizenship Art
Religion	– research or hear stories about religions and the introduction of Christianity. Make deductions about influence and role, e.g. wall paintings, mosaics, archaeology. Stories of martyrs and local saints. Creative writing on lives of early Christians. N.B. Stress most life remained Celtic and rural. Often old beliefs and features co-existed with Romans.	1, 3, 5, 6, 7			Religious education

Main investigations	Key content	Pupil experiences	Differentiation	Key Elements	Assessment opportunities	Links
6 Why did the Romans not stay forever?	Chronology	Investigate and mark on timeline. Tasks based on timeline.	3, 4, 7	1a, 2c	B	Maths
	Reasons – raids, revolts, problems in Rome	Investigate what happened, e.g. from topic books. Imaginative writing or role play to reflect different viewpoints.	3, 7	2a, 2b, 2c, 4a, 4b, 5a, 5b, 5c	A, D, E	
	Extent of departure	Introduce invaders. Maps and sources about who they were, why they came, distinctive features. Talk about sources and how accurate they may be.	3, 5, 6, 7	4a, 4b	A, B, D, E	Geography
	What continued and what was destroyed?	What would pupils have done if they had been Romans?	3, 7	2a, 2b	D, E	
	The local scene	Investigate and list what was used and what was not, e.g. towns, villas, trade. Why were Roman things not always used?	3, 4, 6, 7, 8	2a, 2b, 2c, 4a, 4b, 5a	B, E	
		Use any local information and sources.	3			
7 Did the Romans do more good than harm?	Using previous information	Individual or small group consideration of main changes they have covered, what was 'good' and 'bad', and Romans' legacy. Possibly introduce words like 'progress', 'regression'.	2, 3, 6, 7, 8	1a, 2a, 2b, 2c, 3a, 5a, 5b, 5c	B, D, E	
		Compare different interpretations of pupils. Whole class discussion on differences. Probe aspects such as continuity and speed of change.		2a, 2b, 3a	D, E	
		If time, relate pupils' views to some books or sources.	2, 3, 6, 7, 8	3a	B, E	
		Self-evaluation (on main things learnt) and/or test.	3		C/F	

ANGLO-SAXONS

Topic	Subtopic	Activity				Subject
1 Who were the Anglo-Saxons?	Composition, e.g. Angles, Saxons, Jutes, Frisians Chronology	Map work – where they came from, where they travelled to in Britain and beyond. Calculate distances. Work out some problems faced.	1, 7	2a, 2b	A, D, E	Geography
	Settlement and kingdoms	Make individual and/or class timelines. Relate to other invaders. Higher attainers could research.	1, 2, 7	1a, 1b, 2a, 4a, 4c	B, D	Maths
		Use contemporary descriptions, myths and legends, e.g. Hengist and Horsa. Talk about accuracy. Scope for creative writing.	3, 5, 6, 7	4a, 4b, 5a, 5b, 5c	B, D, E	English – writing
		Maps of different kingdoms, e.g. Mercia, Wessex, Northumbria. Pupils locate. Discuss chronology and mark on timelines. Relate to present-day use of names, e.g. water, police, electricity.	3, 7	1a, 1b, 2a, 2b, 2c	A, E	Citizenship
	Problems of establishing settlement	Either teacher poses problems of establishing settlement and how to organise themselves or use IT simulations for decision-making exercises, e.g. crops to plant, building a village, carrying out crafts. Selective use of fiction, e.g. Jill Paton Walsh, *The Woodwise* published by Macmillan.	3, 5, 7, 8	2a, 2b, 2c, 4a, 5a, 5b, 5c	B, D	IT
						English – reading
2 What kind of people were they?	Evidence including Bede and *Anglo-Saxon Chronicle*	Pupils consider problems of finding out about a non-literate society.	3, 5, 7	4a, 4b	A, E	
		Story and significance of Bede (post 731). Pupils pose questions to interview him (hot seating).	3, 7, 8	2a, 2b, 2c, 4a, 5a, 5b, 5c	B, D, E	
		Use extracts from *Anglo-Saxon Chronicle*, especially local examples. Interpretation work. Discuss reliability. Find 'unrealistic' situations.	3, 5, 7	2a, 2b, 2c, 4a, 4b	B, E	
	Archaeology	Stress importance of archaeology. Reinforce	2, 3, 7	4a, 4b	D, E	Science

Main investigations	Key content	Pupil experiences	Differentiation	Key Elements	Assessment opportunities	Links
2 contd		techniques, e.g. artefacts in sand tray, grids, recording.				
	Artefacts	Use artefacts, e.g. commercial ones including clothes, brooches, urns, crosses, cooking pots, coins, potsherds, spinning and weaving. Ideally access to CD-ROM with pictures and information on objects, or alternatively pictures in published books. Suffolk CC have a photographic collection of artefacts from Ipswich area.	2, 3, 5, 6, 7	2a, 2b, 2c, 4a, 4b, 5a, 5c	A, D, E	IT Art Technology
		Use local examples where possible. Pupils discuss uses and who might have used artefacts. Deductions about the society.			B, E	
	Sutton Hoo	Discuss finds. Higher attainers can use SCHP *Mystery of the Empty Grave* originally published by Holmes McDougall.	2, 6	2a, 2b, 2c, 4a, 4b, 5a	B	
	Place and other names, e.g. days, festivals	Use maps, atlases, dictionaries and reference books to locate and work out meanings, e.g. -ing, -ham, -ton. Pupils try to find patterns.	3, 6, 7	2a, 2b, 4a, 4b, 5a, 5c	A, D, E	Geography English
		Stories associated with names of gods, etc. – Tiw, Woden, Thor.	1	2a	A	Religious education
		Creative work.				
	Stories and legends	Read about 'Arthur'. Show depictions, e.g. films, books, poems. Compare with evidence. Higher attainers can consider why distortion.	2, 3, 5, 6, 7	3a, 4a, 4b, 5a, 5c	B, E	English – reading
	Beliefs, attitudes and values	Stress importance of loyalty, kinship, honour and revenge. Link to present day and personal value. Would they choose to die with their chief? Selective use of *Beowulf* and recent fiction, e.g. C. Walter Hodges,	3, 5, 6, 7	2a, 2b, 2c, 4a, 4b, 5a, 5b, 5c	A, D, E	Citizenship

Key question	Content	Resources / Activities				Cross-curricular
2 contd		*The Namesake* (about kinship) published by G. Bell.				
		Creative writing/role play.				
3 How unpleasant was life for Anglo-Saxon people?	Social and economic issues, e.g. buildings, communal life, food, work, amusements, different lifestyles, e.g. rich nobles, traders, farmers, slaves, women, children	Published books are often useful here, also IT, e.g. CD-ROM on Saxons, posters, e.g. Pictorial Charts Educational Trust (PCET) and fiction, e.g. Kevin Crossley Holland, *The Sea Stranger* published by Heinemann. Also contemporary source extracts, e.g. Gildas, Bede, *Anglo-Saxon Chronicle*, *Beowulf*.				English
		Using structured activities, groups or individuals can investigate and produce a written piece or display on one, some or all of the following. Whole class work could lead to a better understanding to enhance individual investigations, e.g. timelines, reading, stories. Activities might include:	2, 3, 4, 5, 6, 7	2a, 2b, 2c, 4a, 4b, 5a, 5b, 5c	A, B, D, E	
		– role playing or drawing scenes in a great hall perhaps using evidence, e.g. scenes of King Raedwald's tomb (Sutton Hoo), archaeological reports, fiction, artefacts	3, 5, 6, 7	4a, 4b, 5a, 5b, 5c	B, D, E	Citizenship
		– studying rural settlement through pictures, archaeological evidence, visits, e.g. West Stow (Suffolk)	3, 4, 7	4a, 4b	A, D, E	
		– imaginative writing about life in a village or building	3, 7	5a, 5c	A, D	
		– evaluating technology, e.g. timber, central hearths, thatched roofs, metal doors and comparing with houses today	3, 4, 5, 7	4a, 4b, 5a, 5b, 5c	B, E	Technology
		– comparing lifestyles then and now	3, 6, 7	2a, 2b, 2c	A, D, E	
		– stories and investigations of famous Saxon women, e.g. Hilda, Æthelburga, Æthelflaed		2a, 2b, 2c, 4a, 4b, 5a, 5b, 5c	A, D, E	Equal opportunities
		– discussing problems with earning a living, e.g. dangers of famine	3, 6, 7	2a, 2b, 2c, 4a, 4b, 5a, 5c	A, D, E	Economic and industrial understanding
		– examining value and accuracy of source material. Discuss distorted images, e.g. Gildas.	3, 5, 6, 7	4a, 4b	B, E	

Main investigations	Key content	Pupil experiences	Differentiation	Key Elements	Assessment opportunities	Links
4 Was this a dangerous time for people?	Beliefs and values	Reinforce understanding of values, e.g. kinship, loyalty.	1	2a, 2b, 2c, 4a, 4b, 5a, 5b, 5c	E	Citizenship
	Feuding	Stories about feuding from sources, e.g. *Beowulf*.			A	English – writing
	Fighting including wars	Pupils could discuss writing about wars and battles from different viewpoints. Different groups could be given different information and compare their reports or views. Could use IT.	3, 4, 7	2a, 3a	B, D, E	IT
	A case study – Offa	Read or hear about Offa. Characterisation to emphasise his wisdom and cruelty. Discuss what we know about him, e.g. Offa's Dyke, laws.	3, 5, 6, 7	2a, 2b, 4a, 4b	B, E	
	Defences	How might pupils defend against a Saxon attack? Check their ideas against evidence in books. Drawings based on historical evidence.	2, 3, 6, 7	2a, 2b, 4b, 5a, 5c	A, D, E	
5 In what ways was later Saxon life different to what it had been earlier?	Main developments – return of Christianity, St Augustine, other early saints and missionaries, strengthening of Christianity	Mark events on timeline. Discuss changes, link events, tasks on duration, etc.	3, 4, 6, 7	1a, 2b	B	Maths
		Read or tell story of St Augustine (AD 597) – link to present-day situations, e.g. why we have an Archbishop of Canterbury. Imaginative writing on how people at the time may have viewed it.	3, 7	2a, 2b, 2c, 5a, 5c	A, D, E	Religious education
		Stories of saints/missionaries, e.g. Patrick, Columba, Aiden. Use local examples if possible.	1	2a, 2b, 2c, 4a, 4b, 5a, 5c	A, E	English
		Reconstruct/role play life in an early monastery, or conversions. Use contemporary sources, e.g. Bede.	3, 5, 7, 8	5c	B, D, E	

5 contd		Support with selective use of stories, e.g. Kevin Crossley Holland, *Sea Stranger*, *Fire Brother* and *Earth Father* published by Heinemann Discuss realism.	5, 8	2a, 4a	E	English
	Reappearance of towns and trade including London	Which were the main Saxon towns? Investigate if they are still important towns today. Use atlases.	3, 4, 6, 7	2a, 2b, 2c, 4a	A, D, E	Geography
		Read or investigate town life, e.g. crafts, trades, beggars. Use archaeological evidence, e.g. Winchester. Draw houses and streets. Compare to today.	3, 5, 6, 7	2a, 2b, 2c, 4a, 4b, 5a, 5c	B, D, E	
	Coins	Comment on coins. What difference does it make to use money?	3	2b, 4a, 4b	E	Economic and industrial understanding
	Local events	Incorporate information about local Saxon developments. Mark on timeline. Discuss importance of local area in the wider context.	1, 7	1a, 2a, 5c	A, E	
		List main differences with earlier Saxon times.		2b, 5a, 5c	B	
6 Why did the Anglo-Saxons face difficulties and how did they try to deal with them?	Viking incursions	Work on causation – pupils identify and comment on reasons and results after reading or hearing about Viking raids. Use contemporary sources, e.g. *Anglo-Saxon Chronicle* about Lindisfarne.	3, 5, 6, 7	2a, 2b, 2c, 4a	B, E	
	Role of Alfred the Great – importance of Wessex, conflict with Guthrum Alfred's achievements – army, navy, towns, roads, trade His inheritance	Investigate Alfred and read stories. Try to separate myth, e.g. burning of cakes from reality. Creative or descriptive writing on Alfred hiding in the Athelney marshes or other conflicts with Guthrum. Use sources and selective use of fiction, e.g. C. Walter Hodges, *The Marsh King, The Namesake* published by G. Bell, G. Trease, *Mist Over Athelney* published by Macmillan, or Rosemary Hayes, *Mission from the Marsh*	2, 8 3, 5, 6, 7	2a, 2b, 2c, 3a, 4a, 4b, 5a, 5c	A, D, E	English

Main investigations	Key content	Pupil experiences	Differentiation	Key Elements	Assessment opportunities	Links
6 contd		published by Anglia Young Books. Compare images of Alfred, e.g. in old text and storybooks.				
		Decision making – what would pupils have done to secure the kingdom?	3, 7	2b, 5c	D, E	
		Give pupils half a story about Alfred. They invent their own endings. Compare with reality.	3, 7	2a, 3a, 5c	A, D	English – writing
		Investigate and list Alfred's achievements, e.g. army, navy, roads, trade, fortified towns.	3, 5, 6, 7, 8	2a, 2b, 4a, 4b, 5a, 5c	A, D, E	
		Decide if Alfred was a good king. Why? (In many respects he should be depicted as just, considerate, educated and successful.)	3, 7	2a, 2b	B, E	Citizenship
7 Was the Anglo-Saxon period a good one?	Using content previously covered	Individually pupils list good and bad features and make a decision.	3, 7	2a, 2b, 2c, 5a, 5c	B	
		Compare and talk about different viewpoints and reasons for them.	2, 3, 7	3a	D, E	
		Summarise their achievements and legacy. Use terms like change, progress, regression.	3, 7	2b, 3a	B	
		Ask pupils whether it would have been better if they had never arrived. Why?	3, 7	2a, 2b, 3a, 5c	B	
		Self-evaluation (on main things they feel they have learnt) and/or test.	1, 3	2a	C	

VIKINGS

1 Who were the Vikings?	Where did they come from? Where else did they go? Where did they settle? Timescale/chronology	Mapwork based on investigation or information. Show Scandinavian movements – Danish and Norse. Calculate distances and routes. Make deductions of problems of journeys. Infer what kind of people they were. Show other destinations, e.g. European mainland, America.	1 3, 7	2a, 2b, 2c,4a, 4b, 5a, 5c	A, D, E — Geography B, E — Maths
	Why did they come to Britain?	Investigate chronology from first arrivals in 798. Mark key events and people, e.g. capture of York. Some pupils could investigate some events from books. Tasks based on chronology.	1 3, 6, 7, 8	1a, 2a, 2b, 2c, 4a, 4b	B, D, E
	Trade	Use place names, e.g. -by and -thorpe, to investigate settlement patterns, e.g. using atlases, maps. Stress they did not cover the whole country. Their intermarriage with native peoples but also conflicts.	3, 5, 6, 7, 8	4a, 4b	A, D — English
		Pupils then consider why they came and issues associated with settlement. Causation and decision-making tasks. Could use IT simulation to consider choice of sea routes, where to land, raiding, planning settlement or moving inland. Alternatively teacher sets problem-solving exercises based on settlement.	2, 3, 4, 7	2a, 2b, 4a, 4b 5a, 5c	B, D, E — IT
	Local case studies	Investigate or inform about local situation and fit into wider context, e.g. timelines.	3, 7	1a, 2a, 4a, 4b, 5a	A
2 How civilised were the Vikings?	Their image	Pupils discuss any images they have of the Vikings. Divide class into groups. Give sources depicting Vikings in various forms. Pupils write or draw images based on sources given. Explain and discuss that they have been depicted in different ways.	2, 3, 5, 6, 7, 8	2a, 2b, 2c, 3a, 4a, 4b, 5a, 5c	A, D, E

Main investigations	Key content	Pupil experiences	Differentiation	Key Elements	Assessment opportunities	Links
2 contd	Evidence	Tasks related to source material, e.g. inferences about their character and the viewpoints of authors. Use published books, e.g. *I Was There* series published by Bodley Head, *Invaders and Settlers* published by BEEP.				English
	Written and pictorial sources	Other depictions come from film clips (*The Vikings* or *The Longships*), depictions by Saxons, e.g. battle of Maldon, monastic chronicles on Lindisfarne, even Arab views, sagas, e.g. *Jomsviking* published by the Historical Association				
		Pupils rewrite images based on different evidence.	2, 3, 5, 6, 7	3a, 4a, 4b	A, D	
		Talk about distortion and reliability of evidence.			B, E	
		Pupils devise questions based on sources used and others (possibly groups) try to answer them.	2, 3, 7	4a, 4b, 5a	B, D, E	
	Archaeological evidence	Introduce or reinforce archaeological techniques, e.g. using artefacts in sand trays, grids, recording, etc.	2, 3, 7	4a, 4b	D, E	Science
	Case study, e.g. Coppergate (Jorvik)	Can use IT simulations, e.g. *Arcventure III* published by CUP or *Unearthing the Past* published by Sherston. Resources from Jorvik.	2, 3, 5, 7, 8	4a, 4b, 5a, 5b, 5c	D, E	
		Commercial artefacts, e.g. brooches, whistles, belts. Infer uses.	3, 7			
		Zig Zag BBC TV programme.	1	2a		
		How do these support or conflict with images already gained?	3, 4, 7	2a, 3a	A, D, E	

		Activities				
2 contd	Aspects of economic life, e.g. town life, wealth, trade; social life, e.g. houses and homes, food, drink; religious life, e.g. paganism and Christianity; technology, e.g. ships and sailing; values, attitudes and beliefs	Individual or group investigations of aspects of Viking life including structured research using appropriate worksheets, sources, books, IT, including concept keyboard overlays, posters, fiction and other resources, e.g. reference sources quoted above, IT databases and simulations such as *Data 100* series published by Appian Way, SEMERC's *My World 2*, *Just Pictures*, *Optima*, *Redbeard the Viking*, reproduction artefacts, PCET posters, stories, e.g.*Norse Stories* published by Wayland. Henry Treece, *Horned Helmets* published by Hamish Hamilton, *Beowulf* published by Hamish Hamilton, museum evidence and reproduction music.	2, 3, 4, 5, 6, 7	2a, 2b, 2c, 4a, 4b, 5a, 5b, 5c	A, B, D, E	English IT
		Activities might include:				
		– investigate, reconstruct and role play life in a Viking settlement, e.g. York, Lincoln. Use concept keyboard overlays	2, 3, 5, 6, 7	2a, 2c, 4a, 4b, 5a, 5c	A, D, E	IT
		– infer about lifestyles from sources such as pictures, artefacts, archaeological evidence, stories, coins	3, 5, 7	4a, 4b, 5a	B, E	Art Music
		– examine evidence about ships, construct or draw and evaluate technological effectiveness. Imaginative writing on a journey. Talk about distorted or inconsistent depictions, e.g. shields over sides of boats, horned helmets	3, 5, 7, 8	2a, 2b, 2c, 3a, 5c	A, D, E	Technology
		– using sources such as *Beowulf*, imagine values and importance of loyalty and feuding. Compare to today	3, 5, 7	2a, 2b, 2c, 4b	B, E	English
		– investigate and discuss Christian conversions. Use stories, e.g. Guthrum.	3, 6, 7	2a, 2b, 2c, 4a, 5b, 5c	A, D, E	Religious education
3 How successful were the Vikings at gaining control of Britain?	Co-existing with Saxons	Use timeline and maps to show co-existence.	3, 7	1a, 1b, 2a, 2c	A, D, E	

Main investigations	Key content	Pupil experiences	Differentiation	Key Elements	Assessment opportunities	Links
3 contd	Rivalry – Wessex	Research or stories. Decision-making, e.g. tactics against Alfred the Great (see under Anglo-Saxons for resources).	3, 5, 6, 7, 8	2a, 2b, 2c, 4a, 4b, 5a, 5c	B, D, E	English
		Use maps and investigations from published resources. Depictions and representations.		3a	A	
	Danelaw	Maps. Inform about local issues if relevant, e.g. battles, development.	1	5c	B, E	
	Viking distinctiveness – coins, measurement	Relate to current links, e.g. use of dozen and units of 12. Coins and measurements. Number work.	2, 4, 8	2c, 4b	B, D, E	Maths
	Danegeld Æthelread the Unready	Information. Tasks on cause and motives. Who or what was largely responsible for Viking success and failure at different times.	3, 4, 6, 7	2a, 2b, 5a	B, E	
4 Did the Vikings eventually settle down?	Later chronology	Reinforcement of timelines. Could involve follow-up reading, especially on monarchs and key events up to Edward the Confessor.	3, 6, 7, 8	1a, 2a, 2b, 2c, 5a	A, D, E	
	Case study – Cnut's achievements and personality	Investigation. Provide different depictions, e.g. to reflect achievements, wisdom, cruelty. Characterisation.	3, 5, 6, 7	2a, 2b, 2c, 4a, 4b, 5a, 5c	D, E	Citizenship
		Discuss sources and myths, e.g. waves. Possible role play of an aspect of his life.	2	3a,5c	E	
	The state of the country – wealth, town life, population	What makes a country wealthy? Stress later prosperity.	1	2b, 2c	A, D, E	
		Reconstruction using sources, e.g. maps, archaeology, of a typical late Viking settlement showing markets, trades, specialised quarters, churches, etc. Writing on an aspect of town life.	3, 5, 6, 7, 8	2a, 2b, 2c, 4a, 4b, 5a, 5b, 5c		Economic and industrial understanding English – writing
		Compare population then and now. Number work.	2, 3	2a		

						Citizenship Environmental education
5 Was the Viking period a good one?	Legacy – links to present	Stress that the image of traditional England – village, parish church and manor – first took shape in this period. Individually pupils list positive and negative and then compare assessments. Talk about different interpretations.	2, 3, 7	2a, 2c, 3a, 5a, 5c	B, D, E	
		Whole class or group work – what did Vikings change? Was it for the best? Use ideas about 'progression', 'regression'.	2, 3, 7, 8	2b, 3a	B, E	
	Links to Normans	Explain connection between Vikings and Normans (Norsemen).	1	1a, 2c	A	
	Overall assessment	Discuss how pupils' impressions have changed from the start of the unit. Either brief account or what words they would use to sum up Vikings.	3, 7	3a, 5a, 5c	A, D, E	
		Can we thank them for anything?		2c	E	
		Test and/or self-evaluation of what pupils have learnt about the Vikings.	3		C, F	

LIFE IN TUDOR TIMES

Main investigations	Key content	Pupil experiences	Differentiation	Key Elements	Assessment opportunities	Links
1 Who was the better monarch – Henry VIII or Elizabeth I?	What is a monarch?	Talk about images of monarchs. Pupils draw a 'regal' scene. Discuss images and what makes a successful king or queen.	1, 3, 7	3a, 5c	A, D, E	Citizenship
	Chronology – main events and dates	Timeline (class and/or individual). Note main events or investigate from books or published resources (see below). Note main characters and events. Captions or brief summaries of main events.	3, 6, 7, 8	1a, 1b, 2a, 2c, 4a, 4b, 5a, 5c	B, D, E	Maths English
		Family trees – possibly personal linking to Tudors. Can use IT – timelines, e.g. *Time Traveller: Tudors and Stuarts* published by ESM.	3, 4, 7	1a, 2c	B	IT
		In groups or individually, pupils investigate aspects of reign of Henry VIII following structured tasks. Wide range of published resources available. Also posters, e.g. PCET, National Portrait Gallery, English Heritage and British Museum postcards and books.	2, 3, 5, 6, 7, 8	2a, 2b, 2c, 4a, 4b, 5a, 5b, 5c	A, B, D, E	
		For each monarch pupils write brief descriptions and devise a simple set of criteria to categorise into 'good' and 'bad'. Share criteria.	3, 7	2a, 2c, 3a, 5a, 5c	B, D, E	Citizenship
	Main events in reign of Henry VIII – inheritance – character – break with Rome – court life	Whole class reinforcement of main events and some important general issues, e.g. – Henry VIII should not have become King (death of Arthur). – Henry was able but not outstanding, was egotistical and lazy.	1		A	
	– foreign policy and search for glory – Wolsey and Cromwell – local events	– Henry wasted money and men on war and glory, e.g. in France and Scotland. – Scotland was then a separate country. – Henry relied on his ministers. – The lack of an heir was a problem.	1 1 1 1	2a, 2b, 5a, 5b, 5c	A, E	Citizenship Economic and industrial understanding

1 contd	Topic	Content / Teaching points				
	Elizabeth I – character and inheritance – 'Virgin Queen' – extravagance – threats, e.g. Mary Queen of Scots – Catholics – Armada – Drake, Hawkins – Parliament – End of Elizabeth's reign – high taxes, rows, Ireland, begging, poor	– Elizabeth was more moderate and realistic, but still arrogant and extravagant as well as jealous.	1			
		– Elizabeth was keen to cultivate an image.	1	3a		
		– The question of her marriage was a major issue in Elizabeth's reign.	1			
		– The Armada should be looked at from different viewpoints, as should characters such as Drake. The Armada was a close-run thing.	1	4a, 4b, 5a, 5b, 5c		
		– Elizabeth's reign was not a total success; the last few years resulted in many problems for her successor – high taxes, corruption, rows with Parliament, problems with Ireland, begging and the poor.	1	2a, 2b, 2c		
		Besides the investigation, there can be a range of supplementary tasks to reinforce understanding, e.g.				
		– Source work, e.g. using letters of Anne Boleyn, paintings.	3, 5, 6, 7, 8	4a, 4b	B, D, E	English
		– Investigate and relate local events to what was happening nationally. Role play of events, e.g. Pilgrimage of Grace.	2, 3, 5, 7	2a, 2b, 2c, 5a, 5b, 5c	A, D, E	
		– Consider whether Henry VIII and Elizabeth were personally responsible for their own problems.	3, 4, 6, 7	2b, 4b, 5a, 5c	B, E	
		– Compare images, e.g. *Blackadder*, films, with evidence from books and sources.	3, 5, 6, 7	3a, 4a, 4b	B, D, E	English
		– Pupils work out different effects of a monarch not marrying.	3, 4, 6, 7	2b	D, E	Citizenship
		– Write or role play from different viewpoints, e.g. supporters of Mary Queen of Scots, opponents, eyewitnesses, unreliable reporters. Talk about different versions.	2, 3, 5, 6, 7	2a, 2b, 2c, 3a, 4b, 5a, 5c	B, D, E	
		– Look at Armada using a range of different sources, e.g. PRO pack, *Landmarks*	2, 3, 5, 6, 7	2a, 2b, 2c, 3a, 4a, 4b, 5a, 5b	A, B, D, E	

Main investigations	Key content	Pupil experiences	Differentiation	Key Elements	Assessment opportunities	Links
1 contd		TV programme, commercial packs and resources. e.g. *Tudor and Stuart Times: A sense of history* series published by Longman. Pupils look for similarities and differences in viewpoints, e.g. view of Howard and Drake stressing fireships, bravery, superior ships, contrasting with Medina Sidonia emphasising weather and failure to link with Netherlands army. Talk about fact and opinion.		5c	E	
		Sequence events. Cause and consequence tasks. Was Drake a hero or pirate? Use film, *Landmarks*, topic books, sources from England and Spain. Selective use of fiction, e.g. Dymoke, *The Spanish Boy* published by Severn House, Hester Burton, *When the Beacons Blazed* published by Hamish Hamilton, Ruth Manning-Sanders, *The Spaniards are Coming* published by Heinemann. Talk about myths, e.g. bowls on Plymouth Hoe.	3, 4, 7 3, 5, 6, 7	3a, 4a, 4b, 5a	B, D, E	English
		Discuss technology, e.g. ships. Evaluate designs and effectiveness, e.g. *Mary Rose: The Anatomy of a Tudor Warship 1510–1988* published by CSH (can use IT simulation), engravings, descriptions, posters, *Landmarks*, etc. Talk about 'changes'. Creative writing on a voyage. Compare with journeys on boats covered in other study units, e.g. Vikings.	2, 3, 5, 6, 7 1, 2, 7, 8	2a, 2b, 2c, 4a, 4b, 5a, 5b, 5c	E B, D, E	Technology IT
	Evidence for this period – paintings, written sources, artefacts	Pupils use sources to extract information. Look for distortion. Try to get over idea of symbolism and propaganda and why it was used. Does it still happen today? Appropriate sources might include Holbein, Elizabeth pictures, e.g. Ditchley, Rainbow,	2, 3, 5, 6, 7	2a, 2b, 2c, 3a, 4a, 4b	B, E	Art

1 contd		Armada. In groups or individually, talk about meaning behind face, body, dress, pose, background, accuracy, beliefs and attitudes.	2, 3, 5, 7	3a, 4a, 4b, 5a, 5c	B, E	English
	Overall comparison of Henry and Elizabeth	Written sources might include letters, official sources, foreign ambassadors. Find differences. Draw pictures based on differing viewpoints and compare interpretations. Use *Landmarks* and *Timelines* series. Following detailed investigations and other work, class or groups consider Henry VIII and Elizabeth. a) Who was more pleasant? b) Who was more successful? Are they the same thing? Talk about pupil responses to the above.	2, 3, 7	2a, 2b, 2c, 3a, 5b, 5c	A, D, E	Citizenship
2 Why was religion so important in people's lives at this time?	The role of the Roman Catholic Church in everyday lives – wealth– – control from Rome – monasteries	Whole-class work. Stories. Compare now and then. Reinforce with selective use of resources, e.g. *How We Used to Live* published by Yorkshire Television or published books.	3, 5, 6, 7	2a, 2b, 2c	B, E	Religious education
		Use music, e.g. from *Past Times* and contemporary sources reflecting different viewpoints, e.g. extracts from Foxe, *Book of Martyrs* or *By order of the king* published by Learning Express, dissolution of monasteries, churchwarden's accounts. Talk about information derived and bias.	2, 3, 5, 6, 7	3a, 4a, 4b	B, D, E	Music
	Dissolution of the monasteries	Tasks related to reasons and results. Work on sources. Talk about who gained and lost. Could role play – maybe even utilising a local English Heritage site. Use local examples where possible. Focus on different viewpoints and responses. Pictures of monastic sites – how are they interpreted today? Use 'monastic' music and sources such as	3, 4, 5, 6, 7	2a, 2b, 2c, 4a, 5a, 5c	B, D, E	Religious education
			3, 5, 7, 8	3a	B, E / A, D	Music English

Main investigations	Key content	Pupil experiences	Differentiation	Key Elements	Assessment opportunities	Links
2 contd	Break with Rome including annulment of marriage between Henry VIII and Catherine of Aragon	Learning Express's living history video. Sequence events. Whole class stories and reading.	1	1a, 2a, 2c	B	
		Pupils work out causes.	3, 7	2b		
		Stress Henry VIII's loyalty to Pope – 'defender of faith'.				
	A Protestant church	Investigate or talk about differences between Protestantism and Catholicism.	3, 6, 7	2a, 2b, 2c	B, E	
		Class can debate if Henry was right: a) to break with Rome b) to dissolve monasteries.	3, 7	5c	D, E	
		Higher attainers could discuss what might have happened if circumstances had been different, e.g. Catherine had borne a healthy son.	2, 8	2b, 4b, 5a, 5c	B	
	Opposition – conscience and martyrdom, e.g. Thomas More; rebellions, e.g. Pilgrimage of Grace, local issues	Talk about how pupils might have reacted. Use concrete examples of values, beliefs, conscience. Relate to case studies, e.g. local martyrs.	3, 7	2a, 2b, 2c, 5a, 5b / 2a, 2b, 2c	D, E	Citizenship / Religious education
		Use resources such as *How We Used to Live* depicting a Catholic household at odds with Queen Elizabeth.	1	4a	A	
	Religious changes in later Tudor times	Sequencing exercises, e.g. investigation and timelines. Use published resources.	3, 4, 6, 7	2a, 2b, 2c, 4a, 5a, 5b, 5c	A, B	
	Protestantism Catholic revival under Mary Protestant martyrs	Tasks related to change and development and why people responded as they did. How would pupils have responded to changes?	3, 4, 7	2a, 2b, 2c, 5a, 5b, 5c	B, D, E	Religious education
	Differences, e.g. prayer books,	Look at sources reflecting different views and get pupils to note similarities and	3, 5, 6, 7	2a, 2b, 2c, 3a, 4a, 4b	B, D, E	

	Topic	Content / Activities				Links
2 contd	appearance of churches	differences, e.g. in appearance of churches, ceremonies.	2, 7	2a, 2b, 2c, 5a, 5c	E	Geography Citizenship
	Elizabeth's moderate approaches Protestant opponents (Puritans) Catholic threats	Higher attainers might discuss whether extremism is ever justified (it could be related to terrorism)				Economic and industrial understanding
		Stories of martyrs – role play, e.g. using hiding holes. Design hiding places. Creative writing, e.g. letters and diary entries, possibly writing from different points of view.	3, 7, 8	5a, 5b, 5c	A, B, D	Art
3 How pleasant was life for most people in Tudor England?	Evidence for life in Tudor times Stress variety of sources – written, pictures, sites, artefacts, archaeology	Representative sources to give a 'feel' for the period both in towns and countryside, e.g. descriptions, such as those of Vergil, Leland; maps, short extracts from court rolls, accounts, pictures of different types of homes (inside and outside), probate inventories, registers, churchwardens' records, family pictures, e.g. Unton; farming scenes.	3, 5, 6, 7, 8	2a, 2c, 4a, 4b, 5b, 5c	A, B, D, E	IT
		For much of this section, there is a wide range of published material including IT (e.g. *Landmark* BBC series involving a tour around a village, house and garden in Elizabethan times), packs, books, posters (e.g. *A Sense of History* series published by Longman), fiction and artefacts – including coins, pendants, thimbles, costumes and writing sets (e.g. *Tudor Life* and *Under the Rose* published by Anglia Young Books.	5, 6, 7			
		Activities could include: – inferences about lifestyles; – comments on accuracy and reliability of depictions; – imaginative writing; – similarities and differences with other periods.	3, 5, 6, 7	2a, 2b, 4a, 4b 3a, 4a, 4b 5a, 5b, 5c 2b, 2c	B, D, E B, E A, D B, E	English reading

Main investigations	Key content	Pupil experiences	Differentiation	Key Elements	Assessment opportunities	Links
3 contd	Aspects, e.g. houses, domestic life, food, transport, clothes, work, country life including enclosure, town life London, crime and punishment	Pupil investigations and structured activities – either group or individually – on aspects of lifestyles. Tasks might include:				
		– Re-enacting a scene from a house using sources such as pictures, plans, artefacts, written sources. Possibly role play using a house such as Kentwell or Clarke Hall or based on a field visit to a house such as Hardwick, Burleigh or the Elizabethan town house at Plymouth. Discuss depictions.	2, 3, 4, 5, 7	2a, 2b, 2c, 4a, 4b, 5a, 5c	B, D, E	Environmental education IT
				3a		
		– Using probate inventories to draw plans of houses, possibly using IT.	3, 5, 7	4a, 4b, 5a, 5b, 5c	B	Technology
		– Matching artefacts and pictures of objects and rooms to houses.	3, 4, 5, 7	4a, 4b, 5a, 5b, 5c	B, E	
		– Comparing houses and household objects with today and other periods they have studied.	3, 4, 6, 7, 8	2a, 2b, 2c	B, D, E	
		– Commenting on facilities and how they affected comfort, e.g. increased privacy, chimneys, galleries, fresh water, drainage. Using written sources, pictures, statues, memorials to examine changes in clothing. Comment on any symbolism. Compare with today and other periods.	3, 5, 6, 7	2a, 2b, 2c, 3a, 4a, 4b, 5a, 5b, 5c	A, E	Art
		– Investigating technological effectiveness of artefacts.	3, 5, 7, 9	2b, 4a, 4b, 5a	B, D, E	Technology
		– Examining food and trade using published books, inventories of possessions, recipes, household books. Cook or discuss nutrition. Compare products and prices, make inferences about new trade routes e.g. refer to arrival of apricots, beans, pepper, potatoes, tomatoes, turkeys, melons.	3, 4, 5, 6, 7	2b, 2c, 4a, 4b, 5a, 5b, 5c	A, B, D	Economic and industrial understanding Maths Technology Geography
		– Using sources to reconstruct family life, e.g. Sir Henry Unton. Talk about symbolism.	3, 5, 7	2a, 3a, 4a, 4b, 5a, 5b, 5c	A, D	Art
		– Investigating the local community in Tudor times including families, problems. Tasks using sources such as registers of names,	2, 3, 5, 7, 8	2a, 2b, 2c, 4a, 4b, 5a, 5b, 5c	A, B, D	Citizenship

3 contd	marriage patterns, records of JPs, overseers, churchwardens. Compare with today.	2, 3, 5, 7, 8	2a, 2b, 2c, 4a, 4b, 5a, 5b, 5c	B, D, E	English – writing, drama
	– Looking at cases of crime and punishment possibly inferring the likely penalty before seeing what actually happened; compare with today; imaginative writing or role play, e.g. reconstructing a village court. – Investigating changes to farming. Tasks about causes and results, who benefited and who lost. Possibly decision making relating to enclosures, e.g. from point of view of landowners, peasants, vicars.	2, 3, 7	2a, 2b, 2c, 3a, 4a, 4b, 5a, 5b, 5c	B, D, E	Economic and industrial understanding
	– Reconstructing diaries of a farming person or Londoner based on pictorial as well as other sources.	3, 4, 5, 6, 7	4a, 4b, 5a, 5b, 5c	A, E	
The poor – problems, rents, prices, unemployment	Talk about what happens to poor people today. Why are some people poor? How are they helped? How do we view the poor?	3, 7	3b, 2c	D, E	Citizenship
Urban squalor	Read stories about the Tudor problems and how they were treated, e.g. History Source Books: *The Elizabethan Age* published by OUP.	3, 5, 6, 7	2a, 4a	D	Citizenship
Vagrancy and begging	Examine and comment on contemporary pictures and descriptions. Talk about ethics of the treatment. How are the poor depicted in sources?	3, 5, 7	4a, 4b 3a	B, D, E	Economic and industrial understanding
	Higher attainers can consider why the government was so worried about the poor.	2	2a, 2b, 2c	B, E	
	Use any local sources. Creative writing. Decision making – what they would have done to deal with the poor.	3, 7	2b	A, D, E	
Women and children	Show images of rich and poor women in pictures, e.g. portraits, family scenes. Make inferences about lives and attitudes.	3, 5, 6, 7	2a, 2b, 2c, 3a, 4a, 4b	B, D, E	Equal opportunities

Main investigations	Key content	Pupil experiences	Differentiation	Key Elements	Assessment opportunities	Links
3 contd		Investigate or read about wealthy women, e.g. Mary Tudor, Mary Queen of Scots, Bess of Hardwick. Character sketches.	3, 6, 7, 8	2a, 4a	A, E	
		Comparisons with lifestyles and role of women using books and sources, e.g. registers, court rolls, engravings. Use local sources. Also useful is Islington's pack on women in Tudor and Stuart times.	3, 5, 6, 7	2a, 2b, 2c, 4a, 4b	A, B, D	Citizenship
		Talk about roles and attitudes. If time, do the same for children. Can make selective use of fiction, e.g. Sutcliff, *The Armourer's House* published by OUP.	2, 7, 8	2a, 2b, 4a	A, D, E	
	Summary of social life	Pupils present the results of their investigations into an aspect of social life in the form of 'A day in the life of . . .' using writing, pictures, charts, diaries, sources and possibly IT.	2, 3, 7, 8	5a, 5b, 5c	A, D, E	English
		Self or peer group evaluation of pupil responses to the above.	3		F	
4 How did people entertain themselves at this time?	Ordinary pastimes – drinking, cruel sports, e.g. bull- and bear-baiting	Use sources and information in commercial resources, e.g. pictorial, court rolls, letters. Compare entertainments now and then.	3, 5, 6, 7	2a, 2c, 4a, 4b, 5c	B, E	Citizenship
		Discuss why we no longer do some of them. What would they have done at the time?	3, 4, 7	2a, 2b, 5a, 5c	B, D, E	English – speaking
	Shakespeare and other writers	Selective use of extracts. Investigate what was written, e.g. Sidney, Spenser, Marlowe. Possibly use ELM *Wolf Pack* on Shakespeare or Wayland's *Tudor and Stuart Times* series	5	2a, 4a	A, E	
	The theatre	Compare theatres then and now. If time, make models. Write letter describing a visit.	2, 3, 5, 6, 7 3, 7	2a, 2b 5a, 5b, 5c	A, D A, E	Art

						Music
4 contd		Selective use of fiction, e.g. Sutcliff, *Brother Dust-feet* published by OUP.	5			Music
	Art	Reinforce understanding of paintings and symbolism.	3, 5, 7	3a, 4a	B, E	
	Music – Byrd, Arne, Tallis	Audio tapes are available, e.g. from *Past Times*. Also Tudor music and words by the Bagenals. Compare with music from other periods. Make deductions, e.g. instruments from contemporary sources, such as Unton picture. Stress importance of melody, harmony, rhythm.	2, 3, 5, 7 / 1	2a, 4a, 4b	A, D, E	
	Masques	In small groups, plan a Tudor masque with recipes using books and sources as necessary.	2, 3, 6, 7, 8	4a, 4b, 5a, 5b, 5c	D, E	
5 Would you like to have lived at this time?	Largely a reinforcement of content previously covered, e.g. rich and poor, religion	Pupils individually or in groups recall people covered and divide into: a) successful; b) unsuccessful – giving some reasons for choice. Share ideas with others and talk about areas of disagreement.	2, 3, 7	5a	D, E	
	Local disagreements Monarch v. Parliament on foreign policy	Pupils look at and judge areas of conflict. Decide: a) which side they would have been on; b) which side was in the right. Talk about whether the two are always the same.	2, 3, 7, 8	2a, 2b, 2c, 5c	B, D, E	
		Pupils make a definitive judgement about whether the Tudor period was a 'golden age' giving brief reasons for their views. Share with others in class.	2, 3, 7	3a, 5a, 5c	A, D, E	
		Test and/or self-evaluation on what they have learned about Tudor life.	3		C, F	

VICTORIAN BRITAIN

Main investigations	Key content	Pupil experiences	Differentiation	Key Elements	Assessment opportunities	Links
1 What was Victorian Britain?	Main features – buildings, writers, empire	Pupils think of places with the name Victoria in them, e.g. museums, stations, streets.	3, 7	2c	B	
		Brainstorm images, e.g. those depicted on television, in books, locality e.g. houses, factories, railways. Discuss whether they seem accurate.	3, 7	2a, 2c, 3a	D, E	Geography
	The monarch – including consort (Albert), court life, family trees	Introduce extracts from Victorian books. Questions on images, e.g. Dickens, Kingsley.	3, 5, 6, 8	2a, 4a	B	English – reading
		Pupils examine pictures and other evidence about the monarchy. Research some events and place on timelines. Sequence pictures. Introduce or reinforce family trees – possibly linking personal and royal ones. Points worth stressing would include Victoria's longevity, the formality of court life, pomp, ceremony, the role of empire, style, ritual and order. Can use sources, e.g. ELM *Wolf Pack*, or English Heritage pack on Osborne House.	3, 4, 5, 6, 7	2a, 2b, 2c, 4a, 4b, 5a, 5b, 5c	A, B, D	Citizenship
	The locality	Groups and/or individuals can investigate 3–4 events from a decade. All details placed on a class timeline. Questions to reinforce grasp of change, sequence, duration.	2, 3, 6, 7	1a, 1b, 2a, 2b, 2c, 4a, 4b, 5a, 5b, 5c	B, D, E	Maths
		Photographs of local area in Victorian times and today. Comment on information and similarities and differences.	3, 4, 7	2c, 4a, 4b	B, E	Environmental awareness
2 How did Victorian people earn a living?	Growing population	Pupils look at statistics; produce graphs, analyse growth possibly using IT. Local growth. Use extracts from local census.	3, 5, 7, 8	2a, 2b, 2c, 4a, 4b	B, D, E	Maths IT

	Topic	Activity				Links
2 contd	Main industries – farming, coal, iron, textiles, railways	Use published resources, e.g. *Victorian Factory Workers* published by Wayland to produce an overview, e.g. what kind of things were produced, what working conditions were like. Talk about meanings of 'trade' and 'industry'.	3, 4, 6, 7	2b, 2c, 4a, 4b, 5a, 5b, 5c	A, D, E	Economic and industrial understanding
		Produce wall display highlighting main features of these industries.	2, 3, 7	4a, 4b, 5a, 5b, 5c	A, D, E	
		Tasks seeking similarities and differences between now and then.	3, 4, 7	2b, 2c	B, E	
	Factories Mass production	Study sources, especially pictures. Talk about why these methods came in and what advantages they had – who gained and who lost.	3, 5, 7	2b, 4a, 4b, 5a	D, E	Economic and industrial understanding
	Steam power and its uses, e.g. mines, factories, mills and pottery	Look at models – discuss how they worked. Look at sources. Infer uses. Examine local information where possible. Look at ways in which industries were powered then and now.	2, 3, 5, 6, 7	2b, 2c, 4a, 4b, 5a	B, D, E	Technology
	Britain as the 'workshop of the world'	Can use appropriate local examples to illustrate how busy the country was. This could include agriculture. Structured tasks using sources such as maps, directories, censuses, photographs.	3, 5, 6, 7, 8	4a, 4b, 5a, 5c	A, B, D	
	1851 Great Exhibition	Comment on the technology. Look at pictorial evidence.	3, 5	2a, 2b, 2c, 4a, 4b, 5a, 5b, 5c	A, B, D, E	
	Local industries	Creative writing, e.g. a visitor. Talk about attitudes by British people, e.g. sense of pride, feeling of superiority. Can make selective use of fiction, e.g. Penelope Lively, *Fanny's Sister* and *Fanny and the Monster* (published by Heinemann) dealing with visits to Crystal Palace.	3, 5, 6, 7, 8			English – writing Citizenship

Main investigations	Key content	Pupil experiences	Differentiation	Key Elements	Assessment opportunities	Links
2 contd	Challenges, e.g. USA, Germany, France, Russia. Other problems – economic, military	Draw attention to future difficulties. Pupils discuss 'what makes a country strong'. Deductions from sources on competition. Higher attainers can talk about why. Statistical work.	2, 3, 5, 6, 7, 8	2a, 2b, 2c, 4b, 5a	B, E	Maths Geography Economic and industrial understanding
		Brief reference to other problems, e.g. naval challenges; poor military quality of Boer War recruits.	1	2b, 2c	A, E	
3 Was it better to live in the countryside or in the towns?	Basic differences between town and country	This investigation should form a major part of this unit. There is no shortage of resources. They include IT, e.g. simulations on managing a household budget and on a Victorian village. There are television programmes, e.g. *How We Used to Live;* packs and books. Source material is available from Philip Green (Victorian Life photographs), Barnardo's (family life, religion, children at work, emigration, health, art, music, East End), museums such as Cheshire, Elsecar, the National Museum of Labour History in Manchester and a range of fiction including Folens stories and Anglia Young Books.				
	Population – migration to towns Irish migration Other migration Size of households	Pupils examine evidence for location of population. Simple maps. Work on rise in number of people in towns from statistics. Graphs etc. Stress that by 1900, 4 in 5 people lived in towns. Pupils can consider why people might want to move to towns and what problems this might cause.	3, 4, 6, 7	2a, 2b, 4a, 4b, 5a	A, B, D	Geography Maths
			1			
			3, 7, 8	2b	B, E	
		Show sources and information on Irish potato famine. Use other evidence, e.g. folk songs. Decision making – what should have been done? Link to more recent Irish events. Imaginative writing, e.g. feelings about	5, 7	4a, 4b, 5a, 5b, 5c	A, D, E	Music
			3, 7, 8	2c 5a, 5b, 5c	A, D	English – writing

3 contd		leaving home; where they would go; what problems they would face.				
		Other emigration and immigration. Can use sources, e.g. those produced by Merseyside Maritime Museum.	3, 5, 7	2a, 2b, 2c, 4a, 4b	A, D, E	Equal opportunities
	Cosmopolitan nature of cities	Cultural mixing especially in cities. Brief investigation from commercial resources plus selective sources, e.g. local government reports, Ministry of Health reports, royal commissions.	3, 5, 7, 8	2a, 2b, 2c, 4a, 5a, 5c	A	
	Local events	Fit local events into wider national context.	3, 5, 6, 7, 8	2a, 2b, 2c, 5a, 5c	B, D, E	Health education Environmental awareness English
	Urban problems – houses, smoke, smell, rents, slums, bad sanitation	Use a selective range of sources to enable pupils to identify some of main issues, e.g. novels such as Dickens, cartoons, brief extracts from government reports, folk songs, photographs. Talk about main images. What should have been done?	3, 5, 7	2a, 2b, 2c, 3a, 4a, 4b, 5a, 5b, 5c	A, B, D, E	
	Rural issues – improved farming – migration – depressions	Pupils study pictures of farming scenes, e.g. machinery, village life. Use directories and censuses for trades, diaries. Similarities and differences between life in town and country and between countryside then and now. Some scope for creative writing.	3, 4, 5, 6, 7	2a, 2b, 2c, 4a, 5a, 5b, 5c	A	Economic and industrial understanding
		Stress though that not all industry was in towns; agriculture was improving (fertiliser, drainage, machinery, railways) but farming was becoming less important.	3			English – writing
	Local issues	Use local evidence of developments in Victorian farming. Could involve museum visit, e.g. Acton Scott, Shropshire.	3, 5, 7	2a, 2b, 2c	A, D, E	
	Class structure	Talk about different groups and social hierarchies.	3, 7	2a	D, E	

Main investigations	Key content	Pupil experiences	Differentiation	Key Elements	Assessment opportunities	Links
3 contd	The rich – lifestyles, how they made their money	A brief investigation possibly involving a visit, e.g. to a National Trust property. Role play an aspect of their life. Refer briefly to their role in government, army, Parliament and empire. Money from investment, e.g. banks, railways, urban property, marriages.	3, 5, 6, 7	2a, 2b, 4a, 4b, 5a, 5b, 5c	D, E	Citizenship
	Middle classes – occupation – lifestyles	Use censuses, family photographs, local evidence, e.g. houses for pupils to determine main characteristics. Use trade directories and censuses to work out occupations, e.g. shops, banks, clerks. Maps can locate houses. Stress many had servants. Test using census.	3, 5, 6, 7	2a, 2b, 2c, 4a, 4b	A, D, E	Economic and industrial understanding
	The poor	Brief examination of conditions shown in diaries, reports, photographs. Brief comparison of conditions then and now.	3, 4, 5, 6, 7	2a, 2b, 2c, 4a, 4b	A, D	Citizenship
	Children Role of women	A wide range of source material exists, e.g. ELM Junior Factpacks on Woman and Work in 19th Century Britain, *Victorian Britain* or *A Child in Victorian Britain* published by Wayland. *The Victorians* published by John Murray is mostly structured around the experiences of a range of children. Also Barnardo's packs on schools, e.g. *Could Do Better* published by Charlotte Mason, College, museums, e.g. Victorian schoolrooms at Armley Mills and Ironbridge, artefacts, e.g. commercial ones such as toys, slates and pencils, games and clothes, and fiction, e.g. Anglia Young Books *The Mansion and The Mill, Victorian Life and Escape from the Workhouse.* Activities could include: – A case study of a Victorian woman, investigating difficulties, attitudes and how these were overcome. Several books exist	5, 6 3, 5, 6, 7	 2a, 2b, 2c, 4a, 4b, 5a, 5c	 A, D, E	 Equal opportunities

	Topic	Activity				Cross-curricular
3 contd		on Florence Nightingale (e.g. *People who have helped the world* series: *Florence Nightingale* published by Exley and *Florence Nightingale Great Lives* series by Wayland) but there are many other alternatives.				
		– Investigate opportunities for women using sources, e.g. censuses, directories, autobiographies (e.g. Mary Hughes).	3, 5, 7, 8	4a, 4b	B, E	Economic and industrial understanding
		– Look at sources to examine why women and children were needed in mills and factories. Talk about lifestyles and why parents wanted their children to work.	3, 4, 6, 7	2a, 2b, 4a, 4b, 5a, 5b, 5c	B, D, E	
		– Stories of Victorian children, their lives, school, leisure. Reconstruct a typical school day using sources such as alphabet books, log books, photographs, punishment books; compare school life then and now. Use local examples where possible. Can include Sunday Schools.	3, 5, 6, 7, 8	2a, 2b, 2c, 4a, 4b, 5a, 5c	A, D, E	
		– Look carefully at sources for signs of exaggerate. Why people would exaggerate, e.g. Shaftesbury, child labour pictures in royal commission reports.	3, 4, 5, 7	3a, 4a, 4b	B, E	
		Can use selected extracts, e.g. Kingsley, *The Water Babies*.	8	4a		English – reading
	Shops	Use sources such as advertisements, photographs, reconstructions to compare shops then and now.	3, 5, 7	2c, 4a, 4b, 5a, 5b, 5c	B, D, E	Economic and industrial understanding
		Compare high streets then and now in terms of changes of shops. Discuss reasons for change.	3, 5, 7	2a, 2b, 2c	A, D, E	Economic and industrial understanding
		Comment on depictions in advertisements in Victorian newspapers and directories.	2, 7	3a	B, E	
	Health – diseases including cholera – medical improvements	Talk about ways in which we are kept healthy today. List main diseases and how they are treated.	1	2c	A	Health education
		Use sources including statistics to compare main illnesses now and then. Possibly details of ages of death etc. from graveyard surveys	3, 5, 7	2a, 2b, 2c, 4a, 4b	D, E	Maths

Main investigations	Key content	Pupil experiences	Differentiation	Key Elements	Assessment opportunities	Links
3 contd		Stories of medical improvers, e.g. Lister, Simpson. Imaginative work on going into hospital for an operation in Victorian times. Investigate some of main improvements. Role of science and technology. Mark on timeline. Consider why the improvements happened. Higher attainers might consider why some opposed improvements.	3, 5, 6, 7 2, 8	2a, 2b, 2c 4a, 4b 1a, 2b	A, B, E	Health education Science
	Crime and punishment – crimes, police, punishments including prisons	Look at images of Victorian crime – selective use of books such as Sherlock Holmes, films, e.g. *Jack the Ripper, Oliver*. Talk about impressions given.	2, 3, 5, 7	3a, 4a, 4b	B, E	English – speaking
		Tasks using crime and prison records, e.g. details of criminals, ages, sexes of offenders, types of crime. Use IT databases.	2, 3, 4, 5, 7	2a, 2b, 2c, 4a, 4b, 5a, 5c	B, D, E	Citizenship IT
		Investigate setting up of police force. Talk about jobs done by a Victorian policeman.	3, 7	2a	A, E	
		Use sources such as prison records, broadsheets and newspapers for tasks on punishments. Compare punishments then and now.	3, 5, 7, 8	2a, 2b, 2c, 4a, 4b, 5a	B, D	Citizenship
	A day in the life of different types of Victorians, e.g. – royalty – middle class – servant – industrial working family – housewife – child	Using the information already gained, pupils can be grouped to put together a feasible presentation of a typical day in the life of different types of Victorians. Pupils can use a range of sources, including photographs, plans, letters, diaries, artefacts, alongside published resources. They can be encouraged to present it in a range of appropriate forms, e.g. displays, role plays, IT, extended writing, diaries, timelines, furnishing doll's house.	2, 5, 6, 7	2a, 2b, 2c, 4a, 4b, 5a, 5b, 5c	A, D, E	

Unit	Section	Activity				Links
3 contd		Issues they might consider: – rooms in houses, artefacts and furnishings; – tasks for men, women and children;		4a, 4b, 5a		
		– clothes, heating, lighting, cooking (they can investigate menus and Victorian cookbooks), storage;		2a, 2b, 2c, 5a	B, D, E	Technology
		– ways in which household tasks differ today, e.g. washing, ironing, making fires;		2a, 2b, 2c	B, D, E	Technology
		– ways in which homes are different from those of other periods studied, e.g. Roman, Tudor. Place artefacts on timelines. Talk about speed and nature of changes.		2a, 2b, 2c, 1a		
		When groups present their reconstruction, pupils should interrogate the presenters.	2, 3, 7	4b	D, E	English – speaking/listening
4 Why did nobody help the poor?	'Two Nations'	The aim of this investigation is to get pupils to question whether the issue raised is a valid one. Talk briefly about the idea of 'Two Nations'	1	2a	A	Economic and industrial understanding
	Chadwick Shaftesbury	Either stories, reading or brief investigation of lives. Pupils can list what they each did to help poor. Can use sources.	3, 5, 6, 7	2a, 2b, 2e, 5a	A, B, E	
		Pupils can say whom they prefer and who did most to help the poor.	3, 7, 8	2b	D, E	
	Victorian beliefs	Talk about whether pupils think people are responsible for what happens to them. Higher attainers could be introduced to term 'laissez faire'.	2, 3, 7	2a, 5b	E	Citizenship
	Causes	Pupils then consider how people are or become poor, talking about aspects such as money, land, intelligence, hard work, health, crime, famine.	3, 7	2b, 2c	B, E	
	Workhouses	Use sources, preferably local, to tell what was likely to happen to people in workhouses and what type of place they were, e.g. admission registers, guardian, medical. What would they have done if they had been poor? Discuss why workhouses were so loathed.	2, 3, 5, 7	4a, 4b, 5a, 5b, 5c	A, D, E	

Main investigations	Key content	Pupil experiences	Differentiation	Key Elements	Assessment opportunities	Links
4 contd		Compare popular images such as *Oliver Twist* or Patricia Bernard, *Escape from the Workhouse* published by Anglia Young Books.	3, 5, 6, 7, 8	3a, 4a, 4b	B, D, E	Citizenship English – reading
		Sequence and discuss different ways of treating the poor, e.g. Tudor, today. Discuss how and why things have changed.	3, 4, 7	1a, 1b, 2a, 2b, 2c	A, B, D	
5 How did *Victorians* occupy themselves when not at work?	'Leisure time' Class differences	How do people spend their 'free' time today? When do people have 'free' time? See, e.g. *Victorian England* by Alison and Michael Bagenal published by Longman. What kinds of people do particular leisure activities, e.g. by class, gender?	3, 7	2c	A, E	Careers
			3, 4, 7	2a	A, E	
	Types of Victorian leisure, e.g. parks, libraries, baths, music halls, popular newspapers, sport	Show pictures of leisure activities at different times. Sequence and comment. Divide into classes. Stress that there was no real leisure time before 1880s.	2, 3, 5, 6, 7	1a, 1b, 2a, 4a, 4b, 5a	B, D, E	
		Structured tasks and investigations on particular leisure and cultural activities. These might include: – Use maps and Victorian directories to look at local leisure facilities. Link to surviving buildings.	5, 7	2c, 4a, 4b, 5a	B, D	Environmental awareness Geography
		– Study content of a local newspaper.	3, 5, 7	4a	A	
		– Investigate history of a local leisure activity, e.g. local football team, theatre.	3, 5, 7, 8	4a, 4b, 5a, 5b	A, D, E	
		– Listen and respond to music using cassettes and sources, e.g. Bagenals, Dr Barnardos pack, Suffolk CC's 'folk songs and music'.	2, 3, 8	4a, 4b	D, E	Music
		– Role play music hall evening.	3, 7, 8	4a, 4b, 5a, 5c	D, E	
	Role of railways, e.g. seaside holidays Other uses of	Investigate importance of railways using sources, talking or writing about why railways developed, who used them,	3, 5, 6, 7, 8	2a, 2b, 2c, 3a, 4a, 4b	A, B, D, E	Economic and industrial understanding

5 contd	railways	different people's reactions, what differences they made, e.g. buildings, landscape.				
		Pupils make inferences using site evidence, statistics, maps, photographs. Could design posters, e.g. for or against railways, encouraging travel.	2, 3, 5, 6, 7	3a, 4a, 4b, 5a, 5b, 5c	A, D, E	Geography Economic and industrial understanding
		Creative writing opportunities, e.g. a journey to the Victorian seaside or working as navvies building railways, using pictures.	3, 7, 8	2c, 5a, 5c	A, D	
	Celebrations including jubilees, Christmas cards	Look at Victorian Christmas cards. Comment on images. Design own. Investigate and plan a Victorian Christmas. Look at pictures on jubilees. Compare the way we celebrate things today. Selective use of fiction, e.g. Barbara Willard, *Jubilee* published by Heinemann. Opportunities for imaginative work on a Victorian celebration. Infer attitudes to monarchy.	3, 6, 7, 8	3a, 4a, 4b, 5a, 5c	A, D, E	Religious education
			3, 5, 7, 8	2a, 2b, 2c, 3a, 4a, 4b, 5c	A, D, E	English Citizenship
6 What would a Victorian child transported to today's world find most unusual?	Using previously covered information	Introduce through 'time machines'. Pupils in groups and individually use their information to list the main differences between now and then. Talk or write about Victorian 'things' which remain.	1 2, 3, 7	2b, 2c, 5a	B, D, E	
		Pupils think about whether they would prefer to live now or then. Follow up reasons.	3	2c	A, E	
	Stress that the Victorian period was one of great change	Remind them of the major changes in this period, e.g. urban life, leisure, unemployment, medicine, sport, photography, travel, holidays, electric lights, typewriters, gramophones, even cars.	1, 7	2a, 2b, 2c		
		Test and/or self-evaluation on Victorian Britain.			C, F	

137

BRITAIN SINCE 1930

Main investigations	Key content	Pupil experiences	Differentiation	Key Elements	Assessment opportunities	Links
1 How dreadful was the Second World War?	The War in context Key events of the War	Two timelines – one placing the War in the 20th century and a more detailed one showing some of the key events. It may be possible for pupils to be given a short list of key events, e.g. Dunkirk, Battle of Britain, VE day, and for them to research these. Also to find out a few details about the main characters, e.g. Churchill, Hitler.	3, 7	1a	A, D, E	
			3, 6, 7, 8	2b, 2c, 4a, 4b, 5a, 5c	B, D, E	
	Everyday life at home and work	A structured investigation into what life was like. Ideally there could be opportunities for pupils devising questions and talking to people who lived through the experience. Pupils should be given opportunities to consider problems people faced, how they overcame them, their feelings and differences between life today and then. There is an almost embarrassing wealth of resources available, e.g. CD-ROMs (Anglia's *World War II: On the Home Front*), SEMERC's *Just Pictures* and published packs and books, especially Watts *Picture History* series, Wayland's: *The 1940s* and *Home Front* series, materials from organisations such as the Post Office (domestic Blitz, life in wartime Britain) and museums both for visits (e.g. Britain at War experience, London, White Cliffs experience, Dover, Flambards, Helston) as well as loan packs (e.g. Bass Museum reminiscence loan box contains adverts, an old telephone, soap, gas masks,etc.).	3, 4, 5, 6, 7, 8	2a, 2b, 2c, 4a, 4b, 5a, 5b, 5c	A, B, D, E	IT
		Obtaining artefacts locally is rarely problematical – 38 million gas masks were made. A class 'museum' can be set up.	1	2a, 3a	D	Technology

1 contd						Citizenship
Children at war including Blitz and evacuation	It would be appropriate to look at the experiences of children in wartime compared with life today. There are many aspects allowing investigation, role play and imaginative writing and pictures. Resources include film, oral interviews, reminiscences, sources such as Mass Observation, newspapers, photographs, letters, diaries. There is also a mass of fiction much of which involves children, e.g. Nina Bawden, *Carrie's War* and *Keeping Henry* published by Gollancz, Michael Forman, *War Boy* published by Puffin, Alison Prince, *How's Business* published by Marilyn Main, Bill Gillham, *Home Before Too Long* published by Deutsch, Geoffrey Trease, *Tomorrow is a Stranger* published by Heinemann, Noel Streatfield, *When the Sirens Wailed* published by Collins, Freda Nichols, *Back to the Blitz* published by Heinemann. There is also TV's *How We Used to Live*, *Landmarks* and specific resources such as *What Was it Like for Children during the Second World War?* published by Tressell.	3, 7, 8	2c	B, D	
			4a, 4b, 5a, 5b, 5c	B, D, E	English – writing
		5	4a	A	
	It may be possible to reconstruct an evacuation scene, role playing aspects such as crocodile-fashion marches to stations, labels, reception halls, rejection, etc. Tasks could introduce moral dilemmas and conflicts, e.g. whether to split families, whether to return to the city, opposing the war. Jill Paton Walsh, *The Dolphin Crossing* deals with conscientious objectors (published by Macmillan).	3, 7	2a, 2b, 5a, 5c	D, E	
		2, 3, 5, 7	2a, 2b, 5a, 5b, 5c	B, E	
Role of women	Use sources such as oral evidence, statistics, pictures showing ways in which life changed for women, e.g. in factories.	3, 5, 6, 7	2a, 2b, 4a, 4b, 5a	B, D, E	Equal opportunities

Main investigations	Key content	Pupil experiences	Differentiation	Key Elements	Assessment opportunities	Links
1 contd	Clothes Food	Investigate using pictures, magazines, knitting patterns, recipes etc. Make comparisons between then and now. Use artefacts (e.g. ration cards), plan meals. Discuss nutrition. Compare with present day and talk about reasons for differences.	3, 4, 5, 6, 7, 8	2a, 2b, 2c, 4a, 4b, 5a, 5b, 5c	B, D	Health education
	Music Propaganda	Listen to and comment on music, e.g. Flanagan and Allen, Vera Lynn. Discuss messages. Compare with other music.	3, 7	2a, 3a, 4a	A, E	Music
		Look at a range of sources especially posters, speeches, newspapers. Talk about messages. Discuss whether it is right to 'censor'. Use modern images, e.g. *Dad's Army*.	3, 5, 7, 8	3a, 4a, 4b, 5a	B, D, E	Citizenship
	Casualties and danger at home and abroad	Stress that war was not fun. There was much anxiety and many casualties. Briefly deal with casualties at home and in the fighting (it would be worth stressing the part played by foreign and Commonwealth people).	1	2a, 2b	A	
		Dangers at home – creative writing on dangers; pupils can work on reasons for measures, e.g. remove road signs, blackouts, shelters. Design their own measures.	3, 4, 6, 7	2b, 5a, 5b, 5c	B, D	
	Surviving evidence	Brief investigation with maps on surviving legacy of war, e.g. pill boxes, local airfields, bomb sites, graves, loss of iron railings.	3, 5, 7, 8	4a, 4b, 5a, 5b, 5c	A	Environmental awareness Geography
2 Did the War make much difference to what was happening in Britain?	Key changes – political – economic – social – cultural	Using a range of sources and timelines, pupils investigate and note some of the main changes and developments. There is clearly a need to be selective but the emphasis would be on similarities and differences pre-and post-War.				

2 contd	Topic					
		Use can be made of a range of published resources, e.g. CD-ROM using photographs from *The Times*, *Landmarks* IT program and. *Changing Times* published by News Multimedia and Britain since 1930: *Landmarks* series published by Longman Logotron Packs, e.g. SCIP *Working People* (photopack 1900–50).	2, 3, 5, 6, 7, 8	2a, 2b, 2c, 5a, 5c	A, D, E	English Economic and industrial understanding
	Example: the depression of the 1930s	Investigate specific events possibly in groups, focusing on what happened, why it happened and how they would have handled the situation if they had been in charge, e.g: – 1930s depression. Local case study. Look at images, e.g. films, stories such as Orwell and pictures. Other sources might include Warwick Arts Centre/Post Office *A Change for the Better? Britain in the 1930s* or Suffolk CC *Farming in Suffolk in the 1930s* video and photos. What was life like? Was it bad for everyone? Possible visits to industrial museums, e.g. Beamish. It would be worth stressing contrasts, e.g. north v. south. List people who gained and those who lost. Compare with today. Descriptive writing.	2, 3, 5, 6, 7	2a, 2b, 2c, 3a, 4a, 4b, 5a, 5b, 5c	A, B, D, E	Careers
		– Story of the Abdication Crisis. What do pupils think should have happened to Edward VIII and Mrs Simpson?	2, 3, 7	2a, 2b, 2c, 3a, 4a, 4b	A, D, E	
	Government changes, Churchill	The career of a leading person, e.g. Winston Churchill. Character and personality. Why was he not elected in 1945? Simple explanation of British voting system.	2, 3, 4, 7, 8	1a, 2a, 2b, 2c, 4b, 5a, 5b, 5c	A, D, E	Citizenship
	Welfare State	What is the Welfare State? Investigate what difference it made to issues such as health, education, council housing, children, etc. – possibly local examples.	3, 5, 6, 7, 8	1a, 2a, 2b, 2c, 4a, 4b, 5a, 5b, 5c	B, E	Health education

Main investigations	Key content	Pupil experiences	Differentiation	Key Elements	Assessment opportunities	Links
2 contd	Effects of war	Does war do any good? Pupils investigate and talk about different effects, e.g. damage, new housing (comments on designs, town plans), deaths, disruption, debt, shortages, morale, jobs, medical and technological changes linked to war.	3, 4, 5, 6, 7	2b, 2c, 4a, 4b, 5a, 5c	A, D, E	Environmental education
		Compare an aspect of social, economic or cultural life before and after the War using sources, commenting on similarities and differences and why changes may have happened, e.g. clothes and fashion, music, travel, jobs, health, transport, houses, shops, schools, sports and leisure, the monarchy. Use appropriate drawings.	2, 3, 5, 6, 7, 8	1a, 1b, 2a, 2b, 2c, 4a, 4b, 5a, 5b, 5c	B, D, E	Music Technology Science Citizenship
	Pace and nature of changes during the period	From work done during this investigation, e.g. on timelines, pupils talk or write about what they see as the main changes, which decades saw most or least change, whether they feel particular times and events offered threats or opportunities, and whether people at the time may have seen things in the same way as they do. This could provide a test focusing on specific knowledge and concepts.	2, 3, 7	1a, 1b, 2a, 2b, 2c, 3a, 5a, 5c	A, C, D, E	
3 What were the good and bad things which a family might have lived through in the period since 1930?	Different experiences of different groups, e.g. poor northern family, rich family with servants, middle class professional, immigrant, a particular religious group	Pupils are divided into groups. Each is assigned a particular family. They are given briefing sheets and details and information about resources. Each group has to carry out a structured task and then produce an account of what might have happened to this family between 1930 and today. They could present this in various forms, e.g. written, using IT, timelines, pictures, a pageant. Amongst the tasks and are as they might be encouraged to investigate would be: Aspects could cover – the roles of different members of the family,	2, 3, 4, 5, 6, 7	1a, 1b, 2a, 2b, 2c, 4a, 4b, 5a, 5b, 5c	A, B, D, E	IT
				1a, 2a, 2b, 2c,	A, D, E	Citizenship

3 contd	Content	Numbers	Codes	Letters	Cross-curricular links
– changing family roles and attitudes	– changing roles and attitudes;		4a, 4b, 5a		Equal opportunities
	– domestic life, household chores, technological developments, e.g. gadgets;		1a, 2a, 2b, 2c, 4a, 4b, 5a	B	Technology
	– changes to food, cooking, packaging, shopping, clothes;				Health education
	– tasks on changing status of women linked to factors such as education, jobs;				
	– family characteristics, e.g. investigate size of families;				
– school and work	– changes at school and work, e.g. types of school, lessons, behaviour, types of work, economic highs and lows, unemployment;		4a, 4b, 4c	A, D, E	Careers
– travel and transport	– investigate rise of car and other methods of travel;		1a, 2a, 2b, 2c, 4a, 4b, 5a		Geography
– medical and technological changes	– sequence technological objects, e.g. electrical, lighting, radio, television;		2a, 2b, 2c, 4a, 4b, 5a	B	Technology
– leisure	– holidays, sports, music, what money was spent on;		1a, 2b, 2c, 4a, 4b, 5a	A, D, E	Music
– environment	– houses, pubs, garages, hospitals, shops, street furniture, public utilities, pollution;		1a, 2a, 2b, 2c, 4a, 4b, 5a		Economic and industrial understanding
– recent developments	– rise in number of elderly, town development, crime, pollution, unemployment, racial issues, Northern Ireland.		1a, 2a, 2b, 2c, 4a, 4b, 5a 2a, 2b, 4a, 4b, 5a		Equal opportunities Environmental education
	Pupils should be encouraged to base their reconstructions on evidence, e.g. oral interviews with people (groups might devise questionnaires), sources such as photographs (use pupils' families), written documents, e.g. log books, newspapers, guides, catalogues, adverts, magazines, brochures, maps, films (e.g. *A Year to Remember* series) TV (e.g. *Landmarks* and *How We Used to Live*), museums (e.g. social history, theme museums, such as the Opie Museum of packaging at Gloucester, technology museums, e.g. Birmingham,	2, 3, 5, 6, 7			English

Main investigations	Key content	Pupil experiences	Differentiation	Key Elements	Assessment opportunities	Links
3 contd		Manchester, Science Museum, London). Also local trails. Useful published resources include PCET posters; *Picture History* series; *When I Was Young* series both published by Watts; Wayland's decade series and *A Family* in the series.				
		The teacher will need to structure investigations, help summarise key changes, challenge pupils to discuss issues, e.g. compare across decades, discuss what choices were available to families.	2, 3, 4, 7, 8	1a, 1b, 2a, 2b, 2c, 5a, 5c	A, B, D, E	
		When pupils produce their 'reconstruction', other groups should be able to question them on aspects of it.	2, 3, 7	4b, 5a, 5c	D, E	
4 Would you rather be alive now or at the time your parents or grandparents were young?	Summarising using previously acquired information	Talk about what makes a 'good life'. Lead pupils to think of several dimensions, e.g. social, economic, technological, cultural, environmental.	3, 7		A	
		Pupils list pros and cons of now and then. Share ideas. Follow up questions, e.g. what have been the real achievements in Britain? (They include medicine, bridges and tunnels, Concorde, high speed trains, computers.)	2, 3, 7	2a, 2b, 2c, 5a, 5c	A, E	Technology
			2, 7, 8	2a, 2b	E	
		Feelings about the 'pace of change'. Link to other periods of history they have studied. Have things changed in a person's life as much as in the past, e.g. Romans, Greeks, Tudors?	2, 3, 4, 7, 8	1a, 1b, 2b, 2c	B, D, E	
		Test and/or self-evaluation.			C/F	

ANCIENT GREECE

Main investigations	Key content	Pupil experiences	Differentiation	Key Elements	Assessment opportunities	Links
1 Who were the Ancient Greeks?	Greece today – location, features, geography	Look at travel brochures, magazines, maps, etc. Use pupils' own knowledge and understanding. Talk about weather, measure distances.	3, 7		A, D, E	Geography Maths
		Points worth stressing include the closeness of all places to the sea, the many islands, valleys and plains and resulting communication problems.	1	2c		
		Talk or write about images of Greece.	3, 7		A, E	
	Historical background – Hellenes, distinctive but separate units sharing a common language	Pupils think about why people might have wanted to settle in Greece – advantages and disadvantages.	2, 3, 7	2b, 5c	A, D, E	
		Basic characteristics using published stories.	3, 5, 6, 7	2a, 4b		English – reading
	Trade	Pupils could be asked to make some inferences based on sources, e.g. pictures, vases, depicting scenes of Greek society, e.g. stress on ships and trade.	3, 5, 7	4a, 4b	B	Art Technology
	Greek words	Greek words in the English language could be investigated, e.g. 'alphabet', 'geography', 'photograph', 'telephone', 'stadium', 'statues', 'dinosaurs'. Also modern products, e.g. Mars, Andrex, Nike. Pupils could be challenged to find more words. It is important that the teacher stresses to pupils that the Ancient Greeks could not actually obtain these products.	3, 6, 7, 8	2c	A, E	English
	Time-span/chronology	Draw timeline showing boundaries of Ancient Greek life. Need to try to explain	1	1a, 1b, 5b	B, D	Maths

145

Main investigations	Key content	Pupil experiences	Differentiation	Key Elements	Assessment opportunities	Links
1 contd		BC and AD. Mark on Minoan, Mycenean, Archaic and golden age (5th century BC). Stress length of civilisation. Classical Greece is closer to us than it was to Minoan times.				
	Lifestyles of earliest civilisations, e.g. legends – Minotaur, Minoan houses, towns	Introduce through legends, e.g. Minotaur. Can use a range of resources, e.g. Leicester CME Minoan Activity Sheets; IT Ancient Greece by Chalksoft for the Primary Classroom. Several books exist covering Greek myths and legends, Links can be made with archaeology.	3, 6, 7, 8	2a, 2b, 4a, 4b	A, D, E	
	Mycenean features c 1400BC	Can show evidence from Knossos – deductions about life, e.g. stone and brick houses, metalworking, piped water, drains, palaces, trade. Pupils can make deductions from art and frescoes, e.g. role of women, sacrificial altars.	3, 5, 6, 7, 8	2a, 4a, 4b, 5a	B	Art
		Brief investigation of key features of Mycenean civilisation. Comment and pupil views on the pleasantness of this, e.g. gold riches, slavery, chariots, warhorses, conquest, trade.	2, 3, 4, 6, 7	2a, 2b, 2c, 5a, 5b, 5c	B, D	Equal opportunities
2 How do we know about Ancient Greeks?		Reinforce understanding of evidence so far acquired about Greeks.	1	4a, 5a	E	
	Absence of written sources	Compare with other civilisations covered, e.g. Saxons. Pupils think about what cannot be discovered if nothing is written down.	3, 4, 7, 8	1b, 2c, 4b	A, E	
	Myths and legends	Read and talk about these myths and legends using a source, e.g. *Stories from Ancient Greeks* published by Kingfisher, *Eureka* Channel 4 TV series. Opportunities for talk or creative writing, e.g. Persephone, Bellerophon, Andromeda, Midas, Atlanta, Pygmalion, Theseus,	3, 5, 6, 7	2a, 3a, 4a, 4b, 5a	A, D, E	English

2 contd		Daedelus, Icarus, Jason, Heracles, Perseus. Discuss fact v. fiction. What can they tell us about Greek life and beliefs?	3, 7, 8	4a	A, D	Art
	Archaeology	Reinforce or cover basic techniques (see Romans).				
	Surviving buildings	Discuss and draw Ancient Greek buildings, e.g. Parthenon and other Acropolis buildings in Athens, palaces, tombs, theatres, agoras. Work out uses and who might use them.	3, 5, 6, 7, 8	2a, 4a, 4b	B, D, E	
	Statues	Comment on quality and main features. What do they reveal about Greek life and people?	3, 7	2a, 4a	D, E	
	Paintings and artefacts	Use pictures or artefacts, e.g. amphorae, weapons such as arrowheads, jewellery, coins, spinning and weaving implements, vases, theatrical masks. Can use IT, e.g. SEMERC's, *Just Pictures*, books, posters and photopacks. Also *Zig Zag* TV programmes on pottery and Odyssey. Try to work out uses and answers to questions such as why pottery was black. Pupils devise own questions about sources and other pupils try to answer them. Also discuss what they can safely conclude from sources and what is uncertain.	3, 5, 6, 7 2, 3, 7 3, 5, 7	4a, 4b		Technology Art
	Herodotus and Thucydides	Extracts from work of these historians. Pupils discuss possible accuracy. Opportunities for creative writing, reconstruction.	3, 5, 7, 8	2a, 2b, 4a, 4b	B, D, E	
3 How different was Greek life to life today?	Stress variety of experiences, i.e. not all Ancient Greek life was the same	An investigative approach is recommended. Although some attempt should be made to provide a general overview, e.g. reading, stories, pictures, it is more likely that this will be more effective if pupils, either individually or in groups, work at a limited number of aspects. The aim would be twofold:	2, 3, 5, 6, 7	2a, 2b, 2c, 4a, 4b, 5a, 5b, 5c	A, B, D, E	

Main investigations	Key content	Pupil experiences	Differentiation	Key Elements	Assessment opportunities	Links
3 contd	Aspects, e.g. family life (wealthy, poor, women, children)	– to reconstruct what their particular aspect was like in Ancient Greece; – to state how that aspect is different in life today.				
		A large range of resources can be utilised, e.g. IT such as Microsoft CD-ROM *Ancient Lands* published by Microsoft and SEMERC's, *Just Pictures*. Also books, posters and photographs, e.g. Folens, PCET; museum materials, e.g. British Museum. Also organisations, e.g. Open School Trust, 'Learning about Ancient Greece'.				IT
		In carrying out the investigations, the teacher should ask structured questions challenging thinking, e.g. on the usefulness of sources, why the Greeks may have done things the way they did, comparisons with other periods studied, any legacy, progress etc.	3, 4, 5, 7	2a, 2b, 2c, 4a, 4b, 5a, 5c	B, D, E	
	Family life	Activities might include: – Investigate the role of different members of a family, commenting on fairness and how things are different today, e.g. that most families were poor, women had few rights especially in Athens, marriage was often at 14, life was usually one of drudgery (children and homes), they rarely went out. Use sources like *Zig Zag* TV programme on women and education; Hesiod on marriage. Not all children were accepted at birth and education depended on whether they were boys or girls.	3, 5, 6, 7, 8	2a, 2b, 4a, 4b, 5a, 5c	A, B, E	English Equal opportunities Citizenship
	Slaves	– Talk about fairness and why the Greeks had slaves. Use sources such as Aristophanes.	3, 5, 6, 7, 8	2a, 4a, 4b, 5a, 5c	B, E	Equal opportunities

3 contd					Cross-curricular links
Work	Investigate how extensive slavery was and what kind of work slaves did. Famous slaves, e.g. Æsop. Use stories. – Investigate, role play or write about different work done by Greeks, e.g. farmers, teachers, sculptors, professional sportsmen, philosophers, mathematicians, slaves in silver mines. Use Xenophon's *Memorabilia* for Greek attitudes to work. PCET pictorial evidence on fisherman and shoemaker.	2, 3, 5, 6, 7	2a, 2b, 2c, 4a, 4b, 5a, 5b, 5c	A, B	Economic and industrial understanding
Trade, ships and the sea	– Maps. Talk or write about where Greeks went and what they traded in, e.g. ivory and gems. Greek attitudes to trade (many thought it beneath them). Look at pictures of Greek boats. Evaluate technology. Use legends connected with sea, e.g. Jason (can use and comment on fiction film). Use contemporary sources on the dangers of sailing, e.g. Hesiod. Creative writing on perils of a sea voyage and cargoes. Compare ships and trade with other periods covered, e.g. Vikings, as well as today.	3, 5, 6, 7, 8	2a, 2b, 2c, 4a, 4b, 5a, 5b, 5c	A, D, E	Geography Technology Economic and industrial understanding
Towns and buildings	Look at major buildings in towns. Reconstruct and imagine life there, e.g. Athenian agora (market place) with shops selling lamps, pots, vases, leather. Talk about what other products were sold. Investigate, plan, draw and 'furnish' houses. Stress the common use of sun-baked mud bricks, small windows and wooden shutters. Compare with other houses in other periods, as well as today.	3, 4, 5, 6, 7, 8	2a, 2b, 2c, 4a, 4b, 5a, 5b, 5c	B, D, E	
Food	Compare Greek food then and now. Investigate cooking styles and ingredients. Talk about nutrition.	3, 6, 7	2a, 2c, 4a, 4b, 5a	A, E	Health education

Main investigations	Key content	Pupil experiences	Differentiation	Key Elements	Assessment opportunities	Links
3 contd	Sports including Olympic Games and household games	Talk or write about present-day sports. Make comparisons with Greek games. Role play or try out sports. Recreate a Greek Olympic competition. Use sources such as Homer. Talk about Greek attitudes, e.g. competitiveness and hating shame. Compare with modern Olympics, e.g. 4-year intervals. Also compare household games, e.g. dice and toys, with those of today and other periods.	2, 3, 5, 6, 7, 8	2a, 2c, 4a, 4b, 5a, 5b, 5c	A, B, D	Physical education
	Theatre, music and festivals	Extracts of dramas, tragedies and comedies. Compare Greek theatres with those of today. Use sources on music, e.g. PCET 'Music Lesson'; artefacts available, e.g. theatrical masks. Write about or role play a festival, e.g. Panatheniae, a men's symposium. Similarities and differences with festivals today.	2, 3, 5, 6, 7, 8	2a, 2b, 2c, 4a, 4b, 5a, 5b, 5c	A, B, D	English Music
	Government and democracy	A difficult concept but an important one to try to get across. Use classroom examples about whole class decisions as well as those made by one or some pupils. Investigate or role play 'Assembly' in Athens indicating who was excluded, drawing lots, etc. Work or teacher information should draw attention to variations between city states, but each was a 'community'. What is a community? What community do pupils feel part of? What makes a ruler or government 'fair'? Consider Athenian system of unpaid officials, no taxes or police. Is this better than how we operate today? See *Life in the Time of Pericles and the Ancient Greeks* published by Cherrytree Books	3, 4, 6, 7	2a, 2b, 2c, 4b, 5a, 5b, 5c	A, B, D, E	Citizenship
	Beliefs and gods	Use stories or extracts, e.g. Zeus. Investigate a number of gods and what Greeks believed using published resources, also PCET posters and Open School	2, 3, 5, 6, 7, 8	2a, 2b, 4a, 4b, 5a, 5b	A, B, E	Religious education

	Topic	Activity				
3 contd		Trust materials;radio programme of Persephone. Use pictorial sources. Possibly talk about symbolism. Draw attention and relate tasks to aspects of gods and religion, e.g. the human aspects of gods such as their anger, sacrifices, temples, the link to festivals and sport as well as the occult, e.g. omens and oracles. Which god would pupils have chosen to worship and why?				
4 Why did the Greeks become powerful?		List various factors, e.g. wealth, trade, military strength. Pupils try to work out what difference these make to the power of a country.	3, 7		B	
	Trade and coinage	Look at coins as sources. What difference does a particular kind of coinage make? Reinforce work done on trade and sailing. Stress interaction with places such as Italy, Egypt, Palestine, Syria. Pupils work out how this benefited Greece.	3, 5, 7	2b, 5a	A, B	Economic and industrial understanding / Geography
	Military expansion – improved fighting methods	Detect fighting methods from sources. Talk or write about strengths and weaknesses, e.g. Homer on single combat. Draw and discuss effectiveness of helmets, shields, spears and what difference was made by hoplites, peltasts, archers, slingers, mercenaries.	3, 5, 6, 7, 8	2a, 2b, 2c, 4a, 4b	A, B, D	Technology
	Reasons for war	Pupils think about reasons why countries might go to war, e.g. wealth, territorial expansion, self-defence. Investigate or recall examples from other periods of history. What is a 'colony'? Find out about Greek colonies, e.g. South Italy, Sicily.	2, 3, 6, 7, 8	2b, 2c, 4b, 5b	B, D, E	
	Persian Wars – Marathon, Salamis, Platea, Leonidas and	Investigate and sequence events on timelines. Maps and depictions of events. Use specific activities in resources, e.g. Collins, Simon	3, 5, 6, 7, 8	1a, 2b, 3a, 4a, 4b, 5a, 5c	B, D, E	Geography

Main investigations	Key content	Pupil experiences	Differentiation	Key Elements	Assessment opportunities	Links
4 contd	the 300 at Thermopolae	& Schuster, Two Can. Focus on reasons for events turning out as they did. Use extracts from sources, e.g. Herodotus, and stories, e.g. Pheidippides. Imaginative work. Look at events from Greek and Persian sides.				
	Later history of Ancient Greece	Mark on timelines. Investigate images and achievements of Alexander, e.g. in Collins resources. Pupils work out why Alexander was successful.	2, 3, 6, 7	1a, 2b, 2c, 3a, 4b	B	
	Macedonia, Philip II and Alexander	Look at, draw/reconstruct and evaluate the technology, e.g. cavalry, catapults, scaling ladders, siege towers.	3, 6, 7	2b	B, E	Technology
		If done in sufficient detail, some might compare Alexander and his achievements with someone else covered, e.g. Alfred. What makes someone deserve the title 'Great'?	2, 6, 7	2a, 2b, 2c, 5a	A	
5 Would you prefer to have lived in Athens or Sparta?		Both states are well covered in published resources. It may be worth indicating that much better evidence remains for Athens than Sparta. Pupils could think what this may mean.	3	4a, 4b	E	
	Athens, e.g. buildings, commerce, navy, wars, expansion	Pupils could use pictorial source material, try to interpret ruins, drawing or describing life scenes, e.g. at the Parthenon, agora. There may also be an opportunity to discuss who should own treasures, e.g. Elgin marbles.	3, 5, 6, 7,	2a, 3a, 4a, 4b	B, E	Art
	Democracy	It should be possible to reinforce work done earlier on democracy and how it operated in Athens. There could be some thought as to how well democracy works, how it can be abused, whether decisions are always good (the story of Socrates could be used). Pupils		5a	D, E	
			3, 6, 7, 8	4b, 5a	B	Citizenship

5 contd		could investigate other Athenian achievements, e.g. using Cherrytree, *Life in the Time of Pericles and the Ancient Greeks*.	2, 7, 8	2c	A, E	Citizenship
	Sparta – rigour, discipline, organisation	Higher attainers might compare Ancient Athens with other periods of history they have covered (there are close parallels with Victorian Britain – commerce, navy, imperialism, democracy, wealth co-existing with poverty).	3, 6, 7	2a, 4a, 4b, 5a, 5b, 5c	B, D	
		What does 'spartan' mean? Investigate lives of young men, females (the latter had more rights in Sparta). Investigate government and general life, e.g. egalitarianism, communal life (married people did not live together). Use extracts, e.g. Thucydides and Lycourgis. Also Zig Zag programme.	3, 5	2a, 4a, 4b, 5a, 5b, 5c	B, D	
		Other points worth covering are the absence in Sparta of trade, money, art and culture. Pupils might consider whether this is a good or a bad thing. The reliance on 'helots' is also worth mentioning.	3, 7	2a, 2b	A, E	
	Rivalry – Peloponnesian War 431–404BC Pericles	Pupils are told about the strengths of Athens (navy) and Sparta (army). They try to work out what might happen. Then investigate results using books, stories and sources, e.g. Thucydides. Pupils produce timelines and 'letters'/'diaries'/'drawings' of events.	3, 5, 6, 7	2b, 4a, 4b, 5a, 5c	B, D	
		Pupils then decide which of the two was a) more pleasant b) more successful. Share ideas. Would people at the time have felt the same?	3, 7	2a, 2b, 2c, 3a	B, D, E	
6 What did the Ancient Greeks leave us which is useful?	Legacy	Recap of Greek links with the present, e.g. Olympic Games, architectural styles in Victorian buildings. Talk about ways in which the original ideas have changed.	3, 7	1b, 2b, 2c	B	Art
	Philosophy, e.g. Plato, Aristotle	Explain what philosophy is. Cover simply the beliefs of Plato, Aristotle. Possible	2, 3, 7, 8	2a, 2c	A, D, E	Citizenship

Main investigations	Key content	Pupil experiences	Differentiation	Key Elements	Assessment opportunities	Links
6 contd		opportunities for some pupils to talk about or comment on some of the ideas of the time, e.g. no private property, censorship, genetic marriages, rule by the most intelligent and moral.				
	Science – Greek view of the universe	Compare our beliefs with the '4 elements'. How do we do science today? Differences from Greek methods.	3, 6, 7	2a, 2b, 2c	B	Science
	Maths including Pythagoras	Try out Greek mathematical ideas, e.g. geometry, prime numbers, rotational symmetry.	3, 6, 7, 8	2c, 5c	A	Maths
	Medicine – Hippocrates	How did Greeks treat diseases? Creative work on medical beliefs and treatment, e.g. Asclepius. Talk about how primitive it was.	2, 3, 6, 7	2a, 2b, 2c, 5a	B, E	Science
	History – Thucydides, Herodotus	Think about what makes a good historian. Look at extracts. Were they good historians?	3, 5, 7	4a, 4b	A, D, E	
	Literature, poetry	Pupils discuss some examples. What do pupils think was the Greeks' main contribution? Share ideas.	3, 5, 7 3	2a, 4a	D, E A, E	English
7 Do you admire the Greeks?	Use previously acquired information	Individually or in small groups, weigh up good and bad points about Greeks. Were there more good points than bad? Share ideas. Discuss differences.	2, 3, 7		B, D, E	
		Test and/or self-evaluation.	3		C, F	
		Possibly conclude with 'Ancient Greek Day', with activities, displays, presentations, etc.	2, 3, 5, 6, 7, 8		B	

LOCAL HISTORY: RAILWAYS

Main investigations	Key content	Pupil experiences	Differentiation	Key Elements	Assessment opportunities	Links
1 What are railways and how have they changed?	General information about railways, e.g. why were they built? Who used them? How did people feel about them?	Pupils are given the tasks/problems they need to solve for this unit, i.e. – How have railways changed since they were built? – What has happened to railways in the local area and why have things happened? – How useful do local people think they are now, and what did they think in the past? – What evidence exists and what can we learn from it about life on the railways?	1			
		Possible starting point: pupils talk about what they know about railways, e.g. journeys made, books read, models built, sites seen, films seen, etc.	3	5a	A, D	
	Railway scenes across time	Teacher then provides a range of different sources widely spaced in time, e.g. relating to locomotives, carriages, station scenes, goods yards, signals, employees, travellers, etc. Many postcards, books, collections of photographs, films (archive and fictional) and stories can be used, e.g. TV and archive film of railways such as the Settle and Carlisle, Lynton and Barnstaple, Somerset and Dorset. Also British Transport films. Fictional ones could include *Oh, Mr Porter, Titfield Thunderbolt, The Railway Children, Thomas the Tank Engine*. Pupils sequence and place on timelines. Talk or write about similarities and differences. Has everything improved? Why have some things changed? Introduce and use some specific railway terms.	3, 5, 6, 7	1a, 1b, 2a, 2b, 2c, 4a, 5a, 5b	B, D, E	Geography English Careers Technology Economic and industrial understanding
2 What were the main features associated with the local railway scene?	Location Siting of stations	Show map marking 'course of old railway'. In small groups pupils decide where they would site stations (teacher providing actual names). Pupils 'use logic' to site stations and then compare with actual siting. Talk	2, 3, 7	2b, 4b, 5a	B, D, E	Geography Economic and industrial understanding

Main investigations	Key content	Pupil experiences	Differentiation	Key Elements	Assessment opportunities	Links
2 contd		about pupils' feelings over sense and reasons for particular sites.				English
	Main features	Using a range of sources, e.g. pictures, prospectuses, diaries, correspondence, maps, magazines, pupils make a list of some of the main features.	3, 5, 6, 7	4a, 4b	A	
	Support and opposition	Decide if they would have supported the railway. Why? Think about people who might have opposed it, e.g. canal owners, neighbouring towns, farmers, clergy. Why might they not want a railway? Possibility of a mini-debate, posters or letters for and against the line. Comment on reliability of sources. What might they have tried to do if they opposed the railway and how might supporters have tried to win them over?	2, 3, 7 3, 5, 7 2, 3, 7, 8	2a, 2b, 3a, 5a, 5c 4a 3a, 5a, 5c	B, D, E E D, E	Citizenship
3 How pleasant was it to work on and use the railways in the past?	Aspects, e.g. – economic – social	Either individually or in groups, pupils investigate a number of issues and produce a display or some other form of communication showing aspects of railway life. In doing this, they would be taken through a range of structured activities and use different sources, e.g. photographs, plans, film, contemporary descriptions, timetables, traffic and trade statistics, etc. Activities might include: – Work out who might have used the railway at particular places, e.g. from times of trains in timetables, freight statistics. – Look at oral evidence, ideally questioning people who used or worked on the railway. – Use sources including folk songs and ballads to write stories about the lives of those who worked on the railway, e.g.	2, 3, 4, 5, 6, 7 3, 4, 5, 7 2, 3, 7 3, 5, 6, 7	2a, 2b, 4a, 4b, 5a, 5b, 5c 4a, 4b 4b 2a, 2b, 4a, 4b, 5a, 5c	A, D, E B D A, D, E	Music

Key question	Activity	Activity outline				Cross-curricular links
3 contd		drivers, firemen, stationmasters, signalmen. Class talk about the realism of these stories. — Investigate the rise and fall of traffic, e.g. use graphs and try to think of possible reasons, e.g. buses, cars, industrial changes. — Look for inaccuracies and distortion in sources, e.g. an inaccurate lithograph, a 'sensational' newspaper account of a minor accident, company posters.	2, 3, 4, 5, 7 3, 5, 7	2b, 4a, 4b, 5c 3a, 4a, 4b	B B, E	Careers Maths Economic and industrial understanding
	A journey along the line 60 years ago	Using evidence, groups or individuals reconstruct a journey along the line describing features as well as the actual experience of the journey, e.g. from maps, plans, photographs, eyewitness accounts, timetables.	2, 3, 5, 6, 7, 8	2a, 2c, 4a, 4b, 5a, 5b, 5c	A, D	Geography
4 Have there been many important changes to the railways since they were built?	Role of – technology	Pupils look at a range of 'jumbled' sources, e.g. showing locomotives, structures, facilities. Match to dates provided. Talk or write about changes and the reasons for them. Separate into technological and economic, e.g. new or disused facilities, replacement of wooden viaducts, locomotive design, power, e.g. signals, engines.	3, 5, 7	1a, 1b, 2a, 2b, 2c	B, E	Technology
	– economics			2b	B	Economic and industrial understanding
	Surviving evidence	Using pictures, descriptions or, ideally, site visits, pupils produce plans, descriptions, drawings, inventories, etc. of some of the surviving features. Link the present with evidence of the site in former times, e.g. plans, pictures. Match present and past information to refer to features or aspects which have changed completely or partly or continued unchanged, e.g. site layout, facilities, employment, times of trains. Consider reasons.	3, 5, 6, 7	4a, 4b, 5a, 5c	A	Geography
	Visit	If possible, provide a structured activity	2, 3, 4, 5, 7	2a, 2b, 2c, 4a, 4b, 5a, 5b, 5c	B, E	

Main investigations	Key content	Pupil experiences	Differentiation	Key Elements	Assessment opportunities	Links
4 contd		based on a visit to a specialist museum, e.g. National Railway Museum at York, or a preserved line. Discuss museum displays and images. Follow up with role play or creative writing to try to evoke atmosphere of travel.	1 3, 7, 8	2a, 3a, 4a, 4b, 5a, 5b, 5c	A, D	English – writing, drama
5 What would you include in a 'museum' display on the local railway?	Pupils use previously acquired knowledge and ideas	Teacher explains that groups have to plan a small museum exhibition showing what they feel best depicts the main features, as well as providing interest and variety. Some ideas could be provided where appropriate, e.g. types of artefacts, written features, activities such as quizzes.	2, 3	3a, 5a, 5b, 5c	A, D	English
		Pupils in their groups brainstorm their 'display'. Depending on time, some could produce drawings, diagrams, captions, specific lists, explanation boards. All groups must have at least a plan of what they would have and how it would be organised. IT could be used.	2, 3, 7, 8			IT
		Different groups share ideas and discuss the quality of the different 'exhibitions'.	3	3a	D, E	
		Informal test based on 'problems' posed at the beginning of the unit.	3		C	
		Self-evaluation.	3		F	
		Invite parents and others to see some of the pupils' work. Compare perceptions of pupils with those of people who knew the railway in former times.	2, 3, 7	2a, 3a, 4a	A, D, E	English

ANCIENT EGYPT

Main investigations	Key content	Pupil experiences	Differentiation	Key Elements	Assessment opportunities	Links
1 Who were the Egyptians and why were they important?	Location	What images do pupils have about Egypt? Make a class list, e.g. pyramids, Tutankhamun.	1	3a, 5a	E	Geography
	Main features, e.g. the Nile, farming, length of civilisation (3000 years), borrowing from others, e.g. Mesopotamia	Map work using atlases. Investigate why the Nile was important to Ancient Egyptians.	3, 7	2a, 2b, 4a	B	English
		Using sources, teacher then guides pupils to some of the main features, following up with structured questions. The range of material available is extensive, including IT, e.g. Ancient Egypt by Chalksoft with factfiles and journeys to 7 sites; Microsoft; Ancient Lands, SEMERC's Just Pictures and My World; Landmarks: Project Egypt by Longman Logotron.	3, 5, 6, 7, 8	2a, 2b, 4a, 4b, 5a	A, D, E	
		Keep brief so that pupils focus on a few key ideas.				
		Teacher stresses role of archaeology. Introduce or reinforce basic archaeological techniques, e.g. stratigraphy, grids. Can use IT, e.g. Arcventure II by Sherston, an archaeological simulation.	2, 3, 7	4a, 4b, 5a	B	Science
		Talk about problems caused by lack of evidence. What types of evidence do we leave behind today which Egyptians did not?	3, 7	4a	D, E	
		Small groups plan an archaeological investigation in Egypt. Think about what they hope to achieve, problems, etc.	2, 3, 7, 8	4b, 5a, 5c	A, D, E	
2 Did Ancient Egyptian people live comfortable lives?	Stress variety over time, place and social status Length of civilisation	Timelines possibly based on investigation or sequencing sources, or on written information. Mark on 'Old', 'Middle' and 'New Kingdoms' interspersed with First and Second Intermediate periods (teachers could point out these were generally times of	1	1a, 1b, 5b	A, E	

Main investigations	Key content	Pupil experiences	Differentiation	Key Elements	Assessment opportunities	Links
2 contd		weakness). Also refer to 31 dynasties. Talk about meaning of the word.				
	Main periods, terms, e.g. dynasties, AD/BC	Reinforce or develop understanding of chronology, especially AD, BC. Keep class timeline to record features covered in rest of teaching programme.	3	1a, 1b	B, D, E	Maths
	Key developments, e.g. economic, technological	Can use a range of sources, often in published resources or IT. Pupils detect changes and think about what differences they would have made to people's lives, e.g. change from hunting and fishing to farming, use of chariot in war, development of boats. Look at artefacts. Investigate materials. If time permits, practise and evaluate technology, e.g. hammer copper. Work out uses and users of artefacts and how they might have been made. Besides pictures, a range of commercial artefacts exist, e.g. metal animals, shabti, needles, papyrus, pendants.	3, 5, 6, 7, 8	2a, 2b, 2c, 4a, 4b, 5a, 5b	B, D, E	Technology Geography / Economic and industrial understanding
		Possible opportunities to design objects, e.g. jewellery in Egyptian style.	2, 8	5a, 5c	D	Art
		Think about why technological change is important.	3, 7	2b	E	
	The wealthy: kings/pharaohs, nobles	Look at pictures and images of kings/pharaohs. These are readily accessible in a wide range of resources, e.g. Ancient Greece published by Philip Green which includes royal chariot with pharaoh and queen. Try to go beyond Tutankhamun.				
		Comment on images. Use terms like 'power' and 'monarch'. Using sources try to reconstruct lifestyles and attitudes,	2, 3, 5, 6, 7	2a, 2b, 3a, 4a, 4b, 5a, 5b, 5c	B, D	Art

2 contd

Topic	Activities				Links to other subjects
	e.g. in form of role play, diary, story, etc. Bring in their monuments, palaces, hunting, warfare, treatment as 'gods'. Pupils try to spot how their roles changed, e.g. later pharaohs had a stronger military emphasis.	2, 8	2b, 2c	B, E	Economic and industrial understanding
	Compare their lives with those of other kings and leaders covered, e.g. Tudors.	2, 8	2c	A, E	Citizenship
Religion – mummies, grave goods, gods	Explain how pharaohs were treated as gods. Investigate mummification process. This is well covered in many published resources, e.g. *Landmarks: Project Egypt* by Longman Logotron.	3, 7	2a	A	Science Health education
	Investigate or talk about some of the gods, e.g. Osiris. Share thoughts on beliefs. Creative writing on a journey to the other world. Gods and beliefs are well covered in published resources.	3, 6, 7	2a, 2b, 4a, 4b, 5a, 5b, 5c	B, D, E	Religious education
	Examine pictures of temples. Higher attainers might compare beliefs with those of other periods covered.	2, 8	2c	A, E	
The nobility and other 'important' people	Briefly investigate. Write or think about work and lifestyles, e.g. senior officials, governors. Make deductions from pictorial sources on warfare, dancing, gardening.	3, 5, 6, 7	2a, 4a, 4b, 5a	A, D, E	Economic and industrial understanding
Lower social orders	Use a variety of evidence from published resources, e.g. *How would you survive as an Ancient Egyptian?* published by Watts.				
Scribes and farmers	Reconstruct from worksheets and resources, work and life e.g. a diary of the daily life of a scribe or farmer. The latter could point out the importance of the Nile, the use of cattle for ploughing and products such as vegetables, barley, emmer, poultry, fish and game.	3, 4, 5, 6, 7, 8	2a, 2b, 2c, 4a, 4b, 5a, 5b, 5c	B, D, E	Geography Economic and industrial understanding

Main investigations	Key content	Pupil experiences	Differentiation	Key Elements	Assessment opportunities	Links
2 contd		Talk about food, feasts and nutrition (Wayland has a book on this topic).	3, 6, 7	2a, 2b, 2c	E	Health education
		Look at irrigation. Draw, model and explain the 'shaduf'. Comment on its technological effectiveness.	3, 7, 8	2b, 5c	D, E	Technology
		It may also be worth pointing out that the Egyptians made little use of towns, although Thebes and Memphis could be marked on maps.	1	2a	A	
	Women and children	Using pictorial sources and other resources, examine status and lifestyle of women and children. Relevant information is in Heinemann and posters, e.g. Philip Green. Manchester IAS also has an activity pack with a stress on equality of opportunity.	3, 5, 6, 7, 8	2a, 2b, 2c, 4a, 4b		Citizenship
		Compare with the situation in other places and periods covered, e.g. Ancient Greece, Roman Britain. Pupils might note similarities with and differences from the present, e.g. brother and sister being allowed to marry.	2, 3, 6, 7, 8	2a, 2b, 2c	B, D, E	Equal opportunities
		Structured investigation on one or two Egyptian women, e.g. Nefertiti, Hatshepsut, Cleopatra. See Ancient Egypt Activity Pack by Manchester IAS, Higher attainers could deal with depictions of Cleopatra, e.g. in Shakespeare and films, and discuss accuracy.	3, 6, 7, 8	4a, 4b, 5a, 5c	A, D	
	Slavery	Talk about what slavery is. Compare with the present day.	2, 5, 7	3a, 4a	B	English
		Investigate roles of slaves inside and outside the home.	3, 7	2a, 2c, 5b	D	Citizenship
	Aspects of domestic life, e.g. homes, clothes, food, games	Use sources like BBC Landmarks, TV resource packs, e.g. Landmarks: Project Egypt by Longman Logotron and picture packs, e.g. Philip Green. Make bread and	2, 3, 5, 6, 7	4a, 4b, 5a, 5c	B, D, E	

	Topic	Description				
2 cont		jewellery. Look at toys and games, e.g. senet and marbles. Compare toys and clothes with other periods covered.	3, 4, 7, 8	2c		
3 How do we know so much about the Egyptians?	Archaeology	Recall what archaeology is, techniques and how it helps us. Use examples from other units covered.	3, 7, 8	2c	D, E	
	Tutankhamun	Tutankhamun and his treasures are well covered in resource packs and posters, e.g. *The Tomb of Tutankhamun* published by Longman and *Pharaoh* published by Learning Express. The discovery is also well covered, e.g. Longman has a narrative of the discovery through different people's eyes. Learning Express has a living history video on the discovery of the lost tomb, and Dorchester has a Tutankhamun recreation. Pictures of the artefacts are easily available.		2a, 2b, 2c, 4a, 4b		
		Opportunities exist for recounting the story, sequencing, diary entries, role play and/or IT work, e.g. a front page newspaper report using 'Front Page' extra. The use and significance of treasures can be discussed. Creative writing potential is considerable.	1, 3, 5, 6, 7	2b, 2c, 3a, 4a, 4b, 5a, 5b, 5c	A, B, D	IT
	Writing – hieroglyphics, Rosetta Stone	Think about how and why we write. Look at different styles and types. Investigate hieroglyphs using sources such as 'Past Times' hieroglyphs game. Examine writing	3, 5, 6, 7	2b, 2c	A, D	English
		tools including papyrus and stylus (commercial artefacts available). Practise some Egyptian writing.	3, 7	5c		
	Monuments – palaces, tombs, pyramids	Such aspects are well covered in resources and packs, e.g. IT such as SEMERC's *My World* involves building a pyramid. Talk or write about how the pyramids were built. Problem solving and role play – build without winches, pulleys and tackles.	2, 3, 7	2b, 5a, 5b, 5c	B, D, E	Technology
		Mathematical calculations involving pyramids.	2	4b	B	Maths

Main investigations	Key content	Pupil experiences	Differentiation	Key Elements	Assessment opportunities	Links
3 contd		Investigate surviving evidence and scale. Maps, plans. Try not to look at pyramids in isolation. They were only part of a vast complex of tombs, temples and palaces.	3, 5, 7, 8	2a, 4b, 5a	A	
	Art	Opportunities to look at style and content. Write descriptions and stories associated with pictures, e.g. religion; clothes; music; jobs such as fishing, farming, hunting; women and children; crafts; buildings.	3, 5, 6, 7	2a, 2b, 4a, 4b, 5a, 5b, 5c	A, D, E	Economic and industrial understanding Music Art
	Artefacts – pottery, bronzes, statues	Pictures and commercial artefacts are easily available, including IT such as SEMERC's *Just Pictures*, Collins and a range of replica artefacts, e.g. animals, needles, shabti. Also museums, e.g. Ashmolean, British Museum, Hancock, Horniman, Petrie. Comment on materials, styles, depictions.	2, 3, 4, 5, 7, 8	2a, 2b, 2c, 3a, 4a, 4b	A, D, E	
	Gaps	Need to stress that the surviving evidence does not cover all areas. Pupils might consider aspects about which little or no evidence exists.	1 3, 7	4a	B	
4 What did the Egyptians leave to our present-day world?	Organise previously acquired information	Pupils individually or in groups organise work covered, list the Egyptians achievements and divide into 'good and useful' and 'bad and useless'.	2, 3, 7	2a, 5a, 5c	B	
	Astronomy	Talk about different ways of measuring time, seasons and years. On what are they based?	3, 4, 6, 7	2c	B, E	Science Maths
	The calendar	Reinforce understanding of time terms. Look at one or two examples of calendars. The Egyptian calendar had 3 weeks consisting of 10 days each in every month, plus 5 extra days.				
	Technology	Investigate and make one or two of the Egyptians' technological innovations and	3, 7, 8	2a, 2b, 2c, 5a, 5c	A, D, E	Technology

4 contd						
		deduce uses, e.g. bow drill. It may be necessary to stress that the Egyptians were slow to introduce technological improvements such as the potter's wheel, bronze-making, the lathe. Work out how Egyptians made things.				
	Medicine and health	How well did Egyptians know the body? Refer to mummies. Investigate other medical beliefs using sources, e.g. in Heinemann. How did their beliefs compare with those of others, e.g. Ancient Greeks? In reality, Egyptian medicine was linked largely with magic and superstition.	2, 3, 6, 7, 8	2c, 4a, 4b	B, D	Health education
		It is important not to be fooled by the achievements of the pyramids: to stress that the Egyptians were good surveyors but not good scientists, mathematicians or technologists.	3	2a, 2c	C, F	
		Test and/or self-evaluation.				

Resource materials

HISTORICAL FICTION

Some of the historical fiction mentioned in the matrices from pages 97–165 is available from major educational publishers or major publishers with a children's list. However, many of the books are out of print so the best approach would be to search via your local library or resource centre. There are also some smaller educational publishers specialising in historical fiction for the primary school, e.g. Anglia Young Books. Their addresses are in the address list which follows.

'CLASSIC SOURCES'

The matrices include some 'classic' sources such as *Tacitus, Beowulf* or the *Anglo-Saxon Chronicle*. Many of these are in print as commercial publications including The Everyman Library for *The Anglo-Saxon Chronicle;* Penguin Classics for *Beowulf;* but many textbooks for the KS2 units also include extracts from these units.

OTHER SOURCES

These are the addresses of smaller educational publishers and suppliers, and other specialist resource providers. The codes which follow each address mean they provide:

1 = IT resources for history; **2** = artefacts;
3 = historical fiction; **4** = other historical source material

Anglia Young Books – Durhams Farmhouse, Butcher's Hill, Ickleton, Saffron Walden, Essex, CB10 1SR **(3)**

Appian Way – Tel 0191 3731389 **(1)**

Barnardos – Child Care Publications, Tanners Lane, Barkingside, Ilford, Essex, IG6 1QG **(4)**

Chalksoft – PO Box 49, Spalding, Lincolnshire, PE11 1NZ **(1)**

Charlotte Mason College – Lancaster University, Lake District Campus, Ambleside, Cumbria, LA22 9BB **(4)**

Cherrytree Books – Windsor Bridge Road, Bath, Avon, BA2 3AX **(4)**

Cheshire Museum – 162 London Road, Northwich, Cheshire, CW9 8AB **(2,4)**

CSH (Cambridge Software House) – 8 Bramley Road, St Ives, Cambridge, PE17 4WS **(1)**

ELM – Seaton House, Kings Ripton, Huntingdon, Cambridge, PE17 2NJ **(4)**

Elsecar Workshops – Wath Road, Elsecar, Barnsley, S74 8HJ **(1,2,4)**

English Heritage – Fortress House, 23 Savile Road, London, W1X 1AB **(1,4)**

ESM – Abbeygate House, East Road, Cambridge, CB1 1DB (**1**)

Exley – 16 Chalk Hill, Watford, Hertfordshire, WD1 4BN (**4**)

Philip Green – 112a Alcester Road, Studley, Warwickshire, B80 7NR (**4**)

Historical Association – 59a Kennington Park Road, London, SE11 4JH (**4**)

Islington LEA – Isledon Staff Development Centre, Jack Ashley Buildings, Blackstock Road, London, N4 2RA (**4**)

Learning Express – The Royal Quays Centre, Tyne Commission Quay, Albert Edward Dock, North Shields, NE29 (**4**)

Merseyside Maritime Museum – Merseyside Maritime Museum, Albert Docks, Liverpool, L3 4AA (**2,4**)

News Multimedia – PO Box 481, Virginia Street, London, E1 9BD (**1**)

National Trust – 36 Queen Anne's Gate, London, SW1H 9AS (**2,4**)

Open School Trust – Dartington Hall, Devon (**4**)

Pictorial Charts Educational Trust – 27 Kirchen Road, London, W13 0UD (**4**)

SCIP (School and Industry Partnership) – Centre for Education and Industry, University of Warwick, Coventry, CV4 7AL (**4**)

SEMERC – 1 Broadbent Road, Watersheddings, Oldham, OL1 4BL (**1**)

Severn Horse – 35 Manor Road, Wallington, Surrey, SM6 0BW (**3**)

Sherston – Angel House, Sherston, Malmesbury, Wilts, SN16 0LH (**1**)

Suffolk CC – St Andrews House, County Hall, Ipswich, Suffolk, IP4 1L (**4**)

Warwick Arts Centre – University of Warwick, Coventry, CV4 7AL (**4**)

Select bibliography

Keith Andreetti, *Teaching History from Primary Evidence*, David Fulton (1993)

Joan Blyth, *History 5 to 9*, Hodder and Stoughton (1994)

Joan Blyth, *History in Primary Schools*, Open University Press (1989)

Hilary Bourdillon (editor), *Teaching History*, Routledge for the Open University (1994)

Hilary Cooper, *The Teaching of History: Implementing the National Curriculum*, David Fulton (1992)

E. Crowther, *Understanding of the Concepts of Change among Children and Young Adolescents*, Educational Review 34, 3 (1982)

A.K. Dickinson, P.J. Lee and P.J. Rogers, *Learning History*, Heinemann (1984)

The Historical Association publications including the journals *Primary History* and *Teaching History,* as well as various pamphlets in 'The Teaching of History' series

Peter Knight, *A Study of Children's Understanding of People in the Past*, Educational Review 41, 3 (1989)

Peter Knight, *History at Key Stages 1 and 2: A Practical Guide to Planning and Implementation*, Longman (1991)

Tim Lomas, *A Guide to Preparing the History Curriculum in Primary Schools for an OFSTED Inspection*, Historical Association OP8 (1994)

Tim Lomas, *Teaching and Assessing Historical Understanding*, Historical Association, 'Teaching of History' series 63 (1990)

Paul Noble, *Curriculum Planning in Primary History*, Historical Association, 'Teaching of History' series 57 (1985)

OFSTED reports including subject reviews of inspection findings for history 1991–92, 1992–93 and 1993–94 (HMSO). Also The Annual Report of HMCI Schools, 1993/94 (HMSO) Geoffrey Partington, *The Idea of an Historical Education*, NFER Publishing Company (1980)

SCAA, *Planning the Curriculum at Key Stages 1 and 2* (1994)

Teaching History Research Group, *How to Plan, Teach and Assess History in the National Curriculum*, Heinemann (1991)